Robert Browning's
Asolando

Kirchmair
1883

Robert Browning's
Asolando

&

The Indian Summer of a Poet

RICHARD S. KENNEDY

University of Missouri Press
COLUMBIA AND LONDON

University of Missouri Press, Columbia, Missouri 65201
Printed and bound in the United States of America
5 4 3 2 1   97 96 95 94 93

Library of Congress Cataloging-in-Publication Data

Kennedy, Richard S.
    Robert Browning's Asolando : the Indian summer of a poet /
Richard S. Kennedy.
        p. cm.
    Includes bibliographical references (p.) and index.
    ISBN 0–8262–0917–3 (alk. paper)
    1. Browning, Robert, 1812–1889. Asolando. I. Title.
PR4222.A73K46 1993
821'.8—dc20   93–14358
                                                                                CIP

⊗ This paper meets the requirements of the
American National Standard for Permanence of Paper
for Printed Library Materials, Z39.48, 1984.

Designer: Elizabeth K. Fett
Typesetter: Connell-Zeko Type & Graphics
Printer and Binder: Thomson-Shore, Inc.
Typeface: Janson/Dutch

*Frontispiece: Watercolor portrait of Robert Browning by Signor
Kirchmayer, 1883. Courtesy Armstrong Browning Library.*

For Roger

O, call back yesterday, bid time return!

Contents

    "Prologue"
    "Development"
    "Speculative"
    "A Pearl, A Girl"
    "Inapprehensiveness"
    "Now"
    "Summum Bonum"
    "Muckle-Mouth Meg"
    "Bad Dreams III"
    "Beatrice Signorini"
    "Flute-Music, with an Accompaniment"
    "Imperante Augusto Natus Est—"
    "Epilogue"

viii   Contents

Illustrations

Preface

Because the mid-portion of Browning's long career, from *Dramatic Lyrics*, 1842, through *The Ring and the Book*, 1868, has commanded the principal attention of Browning scholars and critics for the past century, it is understandable that *Asolando*, 1889, his final volume, has been overlooked—and not only by critics but even by readers and makers of anthologies. And yet, it is a more outstanding achievement than several of Browning's earlier books and was called charming by some of its earliest reviewers.

There are only two critically perceptive studies of *Asolando*, both of which are very short: Michael Meredith's seven pages in the midst of his "Introduction" to *More Than Friend, The Letters of Robert Browning to Katharine de Kay Bronson* and Donald Hair's article "Exploring *Asolando*." Nor have critics given their attention to more than one or two of the individual poems. Even after A. N. Kincaid in 1974 called specifically for articles on *Asolando* poems, to be published in *Browning Society Notes*, there were only a few forthcoming.

Into this critical vacuum I am venturing. I am taking up the invitation that Donald Hair held out at the end of "Exploring *Asolando*": "It is the privilege of a traveler to be selective, to report on what has interested him or caught his fancy, without being oppressed with the responsibility of dealing with everything he encounters.

Certainly there is much that I have barely mentioned, or ignored entirely. But someone else will have to write a guidebook for the volume." I find *Asolando* country very attractive, and I wish to communicate my appreciation of its landscape in all its detail. It is my purpose to offer critical commentary on all of the poems in *Asolando*, sometimes descriptive, sometimes analytical, oftentimes judgmental, and to try also to indicate how the poems are representative of Browning's ideas and practices during his long career.

Since this study of the poems has its origin in a series of lectures that I gave at the New York Browning Society in the spring of 1990, I have addressed a readership similar to the members of the Society—that is, readers who are deeply responsive to literature, especially the poetry of Robert Browning, but not necessarily scholars. At the same time, I hope that my work will serve as a worthwhile study for experts in English literature of the nineteenth century.

The text of *Asolando* followed in this work is the first edition, dated 1890, although published in December 1889. For other Browning poems quoted, the text is *Robert Browning: The Poems*, edited by John Pettigrew and Thomas Collins (London: Penguin Books; New Haven: Yale University Press, 1981) volumes 1 and 2. The autograph manuscript and the bound page proofs in the Pierpont Morgan Library, New York, have also been consulted. I am grateful to the library staff for their assistance.

I wish to thank Robert Griffiths, president of the New York Browning Society for inviting me to present the lectures and Philip Kelley for a careful reading of my manuscript and for information, advice, and the prints of two photographs. I am grateful to Betty Coley of the Armstrong Browning Library for help with photographic materials and for the loan of a microfiche of the William Lyon Phelps newspaper clippings. I am deeply grateful to Signora Maria Fossi Todorow, great-granddaughter of Katharine Bronson, and to her mother, the Marchesa Nannina Fossi, for their gracious hospitality in Florence, for information about Katharine Bronson, and for allowing me to visit La Mura in Asolo. I wish to express thanks to Professor Rosella Zorzi of the University of Venice for a photograph of the angel at Ponte dell'Angelo and for information about and material from the conference "Browning e Venezia," sponsored by the Fondazione Giorgio Cini di Venezia on November 27, 28, and 29, 1989. My thanks are also due to Daniel O'Hara for an encouraging reading of my manuscript. To Nadia Kravchenko I owe gratitude for her skillful work with the word processor. But my deepest debt is to Ella Dickinson Kennedy, the partner of my life, for her scrutiny of the manuscript and her wise counsel. I trust her judgment more than anyone else's, including my own.

Richard S. Kennedy
Casa Guidi, 1991

Robert Browning's
Asolando

Westminster Abbey and Asolo

On December 12, 1989, over two hundred scholars, critics, and literary figures gathered in Westminster Abbey for a special Evensong, with hymns and lessons, to commemorate the centenary of the death of Robert Browning. At the conclusion, the congregation proceeded to the Poets' Corner of the Abbey, where Sir Stephen Spender, the former radical poet now subdued and knighted, read a tribute to Browning that included an acknowledgment that his voice had been heard by the literary generation of the 1920s and 1930s: "Like Eliot and Pound in our Twentieth Century Browning understood that a poet can only interpret the modern age by grasping at the roots of its origins in the past—in his case the Italian Renaissance—where the creeds and greeds and passions are to be found embedded or enshrined in values that in the Nineteenth Century became disrupted and dissipated in commercialism."[1] Sir Stephen then laid a wreath on Browning's tomb; other floral tributes followed, placed ceremoniously by the American Ambassador, and by representatives of the Browning Societies of England and the United States, the Browning Institute, and the Arm-

FIG. 1. Sir Stephen Spender laying a wreath at Robert Browning's tomb in Westminster Abbey, December 12, 1989. Courtesy Browning Institute, New York, and Browning Society, London.

strong Browning Library. The participants then adjourned to the Jerusalem Chamber for a reception.

These several organizations and others had been celebrating the centenary year in England, the United States, and Italy all during the year 1989 with musical programs, readings of Browning's poems, dramatic productions, special exhibitions, and scholarly conferences. The most spectacular of these were *Robert Browning, a Telescopic View*, a display of books and manuscripts at the Armstrong Browning Library in Texas, later moved to the Pierpont Morgan Library in New York, and the scholarly conference *Browning e Venezia* held on the island of San Giorgio in Venice and supplemented by a breathtaking exhibition of manuscripts, letters, books, portraits, drawings, and photographs at the Palazzo Querini Stampalia.[2] Browning's memory had never been better served.

The international recognition and appreciation of the genius of Robert Browning has been going on for a hundred years. It began immediately after Browning's death in Venice on December 12, 1889, in an upper room of his son's newly purchased Palazzo Rezzonico on the Grand Canal. The officialdom of Venice made arrangements for a stately and uniquely Venetian funeral. After a brief funeral service in the first-floor sala of the palazzo, which was attended by a small group of family and friends, a squad of eight "pompieri" in blue uniforms and shining brass helmets bore the coffin down to the canopied black and gold funeral barge, hung with funeral wreaths. As the sun was setting, the barge, with a golden lion at the prow and propelled by gondoliers dressed in gold and black velvet, led the cortege of gondolas down the Grand Canal and out to the isle of the dead, San Michele, where Browning's body was held awaiting burial.[3]

It had been his wish, if he died in Italy, to be buried beside his wife Elizabeth in the English (Protestant) Cemetery in Florence, but the cemetery was at that time

Funeral of Robert Browning Dec 31" 89   Scene at the Grave   Sketch of the Coffin

FIG. 2. The burial of Robert Browning in the Poets' Corner, Westminster Abbey, December 12, 1889. *Pall Mall Budget*, January 2, 1890.

closed to further interments. However, his publisher, George Murray Smith, had secured an invitation from the dean of Westminster Abbey for Browning to be buried in the Poets' Corner, adjacent to the grave of Chaucer.[4] The body was shipped to Browning's London home, 29 De Vere Gardens, where it lay in a sealed coffin, awaiting the burial service.

On December 31, a fog-shrouded morning, the ceremonies began with the coffin being carried to the horse-drawn hearse, observed by a crowd of onlookers. There were so many floral wreaths that they would not fit into the hearse with the coffin. Ten carriages conveyed the chief mourners through Knightsbridge, past Buckingham Palace Gardens down to Westminster Abbey.[5]

The congregation numbered over six hundred, including an assembly of the late-Victorian great from the literary and cultural world.[6] The massive abbey bell tolled for fifteen minutes before the coffin was borne in, the pallbearers led by the poet's son, Pen (Robert Barrett Browning). After a chanting of the 90th Psalm and a reading from First Corinthians ("For this corruptible must put on incorruption, and this mortal must put on immortality") came the most moving feature of the program, a musical setting of Elizabeth Barrett Browning's "The Sleep," three stanzas beginning,

> What would we give to our beloved?
> The hero's heart to be unmoved,
> The poet's star-tuned harp to sweep,
> The patriot's voice to teach and rouse,
> The monarch's crown to light the brows?
> He giveth His belovèd—sleep

A boy soprano sang the first line, with the full choir answering in increasing fullness up to "the monarch's crown" and then falling to a pianissimo for the refrain.

The coffin was now carried to the Poets' Corner with the choir pacing to Schubert's Funeral March. After the coffin was lowered into the grave, the choir began Isaac Watts's hymn "O God, our help in ages past" and was joined spontaneously by the full congregation. As a recessional, the organist played the "Dead March" from

Handel's oratorio *Saul* while the mourners passed around the grave.

Although Browning was over seventy-seven when he died, he had appeared to be in such vigorous health that his friends had not expected to lose him soon. His appearance was robust. He maintained a disciplined routine: he rose at six or seven, took a cold bath, ate a simple breakfast, then went out for a walk of two hours, frequently accompanied by his sister, Sarianna, or a friend. One companion, Dr. Hiram Corson, remembered, "He stepped more briskly than most men do in the prime of life; he strode really . . . I walked with him one day . . . and had to quicken my pace . . . to keep along with him."[7] He returned to a stint of two hours reading, followed by a light lunch, then three or more hours of writing or reading. He maintained a voluminous correspondence, for he conscientiously answered a flood of letters, many from strangers or remote acquaintances who asked him about his poems or requested that he read and comment on verses they had written.[8] In these later years, he seldom stopped for tea, preferring to eat a good dinner, for he was invited to large or small dinner parties on most of the evenings of the week. He did not stay out late, hoping to retire by ten or eleven.[9]

But in his last months, he suffered from frequent colds and coughs. He believed in long walks as a remedy for poor health and continually urged his friend Mrs. Katharine Bronson, whose health was fragile, to take this mode of exercise. In August 1889, he complained of ill health to his friend the Reverend J. D. Williams and of the cool weather in London. Just as he was about to take his annual vacation to Italy, he wrote, "I have been able to walk and to keep quiet, to the great improvement of my health—so that I do not throw onto Italy the whole burden of making me well again—so far as 'well' is possible."[10] Friends remembered too that he exhibited shortness of breath while climbing hills or stairs.[11]

However, this was only in his final months. Before that, friends had thought he would live well into his eighties, for they were aware that he followed an admirable regime and that he took a three-month vacation every year. In the last eleven years of his life, he spent eight of these autumn holidays in Italy, usually in Venice, for he avoided Florence and Rome, cities associated with the happy years of his marriage with Elizabeth.

One of the principal attractions of Venice was his close association with Katharine Bronson, a wealthy American whose husband enjoyed international travel and at length gave up his American residence to settle in Venice.[12] Mrs. Bronson seemed happy about this decision. She was a woman of wit and culture, with exquisite taste that had been formed by her extensive travel. She was an excellent hostess who enjoyed the company of artists, writers, men in public service and their accomplished wives. Although of modest confidence in herself, she had intellectual and literary leanings and engaged in serious research and writing in Venetian history. Her life and personality resembled that of her compatriot Edith Wharton, and like Edith Wharton, she suffered a breakup in her marriage in the early 1880s. Her husband, who appears to have taken up with another woman and moved to Paris, was said to be experiencing a mental break-

FIG. 3. Portrait of Katharine Bronson. Courtesy private collection, Florence.

FIG. 4. Ca' Alvisi, on the left, Katharine Bronson's home on the Grand Canal, Venice. Photo, Richard Kennedy.

down.[13] With admirable discretion she did not discuss her domestic life with her friends but launched into a more lively social life without her husband, using her great wealth and her charming small palazzo on the Grand Canal, Ca' Alvisi, to help her take an active role in international Venetian society.[14]

Katharine Bronson had met Browning during his 1880 vacation with his sister, Sarianna, in Venice, and a solid friendship ripened after she had entertained them several times at Ca' Alvisi. In 1883, when the hotel where the Brownings usually stayed closed down, she invited them to reside next door to Ca' Alvisi in the Palazzo Guistinaiani-Recanti, which she had rented in order to accommodate guests, and in the later 1880s, she arranged rooms for them in Ca' Alvisi itself. After the Venetian visits had become an annual event, Browning considered buying the Palazzo Manzoni as a Venetian home for himself and for Pen, who had become very attracted to Venice. Michael Meredith speculates that Browning had hopes that Pen, still unmarried at age thirty-five, might be drawn to Mrs. Bronson's lively, attractive daughter Edith and thus cement their friendship even more closely.[15]

After the death of Mrs. Bronson's husband in 1885, the close association that Browning continued with her led some of her friends to wonder if a late marriage with the elderly poet might take place. Michael Meredith argues a very persuasive case that, as the years went by, Browning developed a deep emotional attachment to Mrs. Bronson and began to make an unconscious identification between her and Elizabeth. On his watch chain, where he wore Elizabeth's ring, he added a commemorative coin that Mrs. Bronson had given him. He told her that he was reminded of her every few minutes when the coin tinkled against the ring.[16]

During the last year of Browning's life, Mrs. Bronson purchased a summer villa in Asolo, a picturesque town north of Venice that Browning had come to love when he first visited there while exploring the region for its associations with Sordello, the troubadour hero of his long poem published in 1840. The villa was named (in the Venetian dialect) La Mura, for it was set into the town

FIG. 5. View of Asolo, with the Rocca dominating the town; on the right, the cathedral tower. Photo, Richard Kennedy.

wall, just inside the arch of the entrance gate. Asolo is one of the most charming hill towns in Italy, with its medieval ramparts, its old houses with faded frescos on their facades, and its Gothic arcaded streets, the whole dominated by the Rocca, the pre-Roman castle ruins on a height overlooking the valley below. From the loggia of La Mura, one sees a splendid panorama of the town: on the right stood the cathedral and the steps leading up to the central piazza where a fountain was guarded by a proud stone lion; in front, across a deep ravine, was the

FIG. 6. La Mura, Katharine Bronson's villa in Asolo.
Photo, Richard Kennedy.

stately palace of Caterina Cornaro, the exiled queen of
Cyprus, who had been given this region of the Veneto as
her domain in the late fifteenth century; and to the left
the wide sweep of the plain with its fields and vineyards
reached toward the River Musone.

In August, Mrs. Bronson invited Robert and Sarianna
to visit and arranged newly furnished rooms for them in
a house across the street from La Mura, in "my very own
of Italian towns," as Browning called it.[17] Every day he
followed a schedule that included clambering over the
hills in the morning, working on his poems or reading in

FIG. 7. The Via Roberto Browning, which goes past La Mura to the entrance gate of Asolo. Photo, Richard Kennedy.

FIG. 8. The Torre de'Eccelino at Romano. Photo, Richard Kennedy.

the early part of the day, and joining Mrs. Bronson in her "old-time, rattling red-velveted carriage"[18] for drives around the countryside in the afternoon. They viewed landscapes, stopped at ancient churches, visited museums, and sought out historic sites, such as the fortified town of Cittadella. At Romano, Browning responded with a nostalgic pang to the Torre d'Eccelino, which he had first viewed in 1838, stronghold of the Eccelini, about whom he had written in *Sordello*. At Altivolo, he mused over the mutabilities of time at the Barco della Regina Cornaro, the ruined villa of the queen, now a farm building, with pigs and poultry roaming about outside its frescoed walls. At Possagno, he was fascinated by the drawings, models, and sculptured works of Canova. One day he and Mrs. Bronson drove beyond Bassano to see Marostica, the fortified town of the Scaligeri, whose walls snaked up to the castle overlooking the region. "Pen must see this," he said. "Dear Pen."[19] Browning seemed mesmerized by his surroundings.

Almost always, the touring party would return in time to view the sunset from the loggia, a sight that seemed to nurture Browning with its beauty. He stood in contemplation, staring at the clock tower of Queen Caterina with its outcropping of weeds at the top. So immersed in the atmosphere of Asolo did he become that he planned to buy a property across the gorge from La Mura, an unfinished school building on a site offering a magnificent view—even as far as Venice on a clear day—and in order to enhance the overlook, he had in mind to add a tower, "Pippa's Tower"[20] he would call it, in memory of his play, *Pippa Passes*, written in 1839, which he had set in

FIG. 9. The entrance gate and city wall at Cittadella. Photo, Richard Kennedy.

Asolo. After dinner, Browning would play upon the spinet for Mrs. Bronson and Edith—and faithful Sarianna, who worked at netting in a quiet corner—and often he would sing as he played Russian folk songs that he had learned on his trip to Moscow in his youth. Or he would read aloud to the company, not his own work, but poems of Keats, Shelley, or Tennyson.[21]

Even before he arrived in Asolo, he had decided to dedicate his latest collection of poems to Mrs. Bronson, telling her in a letter, "I shall bring *your* bookful of verses for final overhauling on the spot where, when I first saw

FIG. 10. Palazzo Rezzonico, Pen Browning's home on the Grand Canal, Venice. Robert Browning died in the room on the top floor, left. Photo, Richard Kennedy.

it, inspiration seemed to steam up from the ground."[22] Now, enchanted once more, he expanded his book and rearranged its contents. He gave it a new name, *Asolando*, as a tribute to his stay in Asolo, which he declared "the most beautiful spot I ever was privileged to see."[23] By mid-October, he had dispatched the manuscript to George Smith in London, describing it to a friend as "some thirty pieces great and small, of various kinds and qualities—not a few written and all supervised, in this lovely Asolo—my spot of predilection in the whole world I think."[24]

The autumn dreamed on. He seemed unable to tear himself away from Asolo. But with the onset of cold weather at the end of October, he was ready to leave. His plans for some time had been to visit Pen and his wife, Fannie, in Venice, where Pen had purchased the grandiose palazzo of Cardinal Carlo Rezzonico (later Pope Clement XIII) on the Grand Canal. Pen had been at work redecorating the rooms and was eager for his father to see his new Italian home. On October 31, he arrived to drive Robert and Sarianna to Venice.

The Palazzo Rezzonico was a magnificent structure of white marble, its purchase made possible by Pen's marriage to a rich American woman. In height three stories, it had a richly carved baroque facade and seven bays of windows across, each set between pillars. A spacious gondola park in front surrounded a gracious flight of marble stairs leading through double doors into the court, the ground-floor reception area. To Henry James it seemed like "some broad-breasted mythological sea-horse rearing up from the flood with the toss of a sculptured crest and with emerged knees figured by water steps."[25] An airy courtyard provided interior light for the rooms. Wall hangings and sculptured nudes from the eighteenth century adorned the grand sala on the first floor; the family drawing room on the second floor had a ceiling fresco by Tiepolo, but Pen had decorated the room in the Victorian domestic style with brocaded wall coverings, comfortable chairs draped with antimacassars, and a mixture of Renaissance and eighteenth-century tables and secretaries. A full-length portrait of Browning, painted by Pen, hung on the wall. Long marble stairways leading up to the sala and again to the second floor, a total of seventy-two steps, made Browning puff as he climbed.[26]

In Venice he was full of talk about Asolo, "his delight in it and the beauty of its situation."[27] He told Pen, Fannie, and their guests, Constance and Evelyn Barclay and Major G. D. Giles, all about his plans to buy the house in Asolo as soon as the town authorities could arrange the sale. He entered vigorously into social life in Venice, dining out, going to tea, attending the opera, giving readings of his poems to groups of friends. On November 19, he gave a reading of the as-yet-unpublished poems from *Asolando* at the Palazzo Barbaro, where his hosts, Mr. and Mrs. Daniel S. Curtis of Boston, had an apartment. He read for two hours, standing, with only one intermission but offered several times to stop for fear of tiring his listeners. Curtis described a remarkable change in personality during the performance: "When he reads his own poetry, he ceases to be the Browning of Society and puts off 'that side to show the world' and becomes Browning the poet, is seen, as it were, under the afflatus by which he is inspired and carried away, and his voice, features, manner then reflect the great qualities of his verse and he is his greater Self—and his own best interpreter."[28]

Every morning, no matter what the weather, he went for a two-hour walk on the Lido. On November 21 and 22, he took his walk on cold, foggy days and caught a bad cold that caused him to cough in a way to worry the company at Palazzo Rezzonico.[29] During the next few days he refused to stay home from social engagements, and his cough was no better. On the evening of Novem-

FIG. 11. The Lion in the piazza at Asolo. Sketch, Ella Kennedy.

ber 28, he went with the family group to hear *Carmen*, although he still felt ill, and he almost fainted on the stairs when they returned home.

Although Browning had stubbornly refused to see a physician ("They are all fools," he claimed), Pen now sent for Dr. Cini, the physician to the English-speaking expatriates, who diagnosed bronchitis but also expressed concern about Browning's heart. He was kept in bed with warm linseed poultices applied to his chest, but at night he suffered coughing fits that alarmed Pen and Fannie.[30] During the next few days, two more doctors were called in and a nurse hired to attend him. Besides spasms of coughing, he suffered difficulty in breathing. The doctors now discerned "syncope of the heart," irregular heartbeat.[31]

By December 11, his pulse had become weak, and he had begun to have periods of delirium. On December 12, he seemed better but suffered another episode of "syncope of the heart" in the morning. He was cheered by the receipt of the first copy of *Asolando*, saying with true author's pleasure, "What a pretty colour the binding is."[32] Other good tidings came during the day: the municipal authorities in Asolo had approved the sale of the property he wished to buy. At 6:30 P.M. a telegram arrived from George Smith about *Asolando*, which was published that day, although proof sheets had earlier been given to the newspapers. Pen read the telegram to his father: "Reviews in all this day's papers most favorable. Edition nearly exhausted."[33] As Pen bent over, Browning murmured "How gratifying." They were his last intelligible words.[34]

2

The Personal Voice

Asolando takes its title, as the dedication "To Mrs. Arthur Bronson" explains, from the playful Latin verb form that Pietro Bembo, when he was secretary to Caterina Cornaro, had coined—*asolare*.[1] Browning interpreted it to mean "to disport in the open air, amuse oneself at random," which was the spirit of his sojourn in Asolo at Mrs. Bronson's villa. The title and its sauntering tone are appropriate to this book, for the miscellaneous poems are the product of an Indian summer of poetic resurgence—indeed, they do not seem to be the work of an elderly man. The mood varies throughout the volume: many of the poems are light in manner, even comic; others are serene. Browning had first thought to entitle his book *A New Series of Jocoseria*,[2] as if to indicate a similarity in mixture to that earlier publication, which he had described to F. J. Furnivall as "a collection of things grav*ish* and gay*ish*."[3]

The final title was decided upon in 1889 while he was basking in those autumn days at Asolo. To it he added a subtitle, *Fancies and Facts*, which reflects an elusive theme that plays in and out of a number of poems and gives the collection a semblance of unity. The theme had been first developed in his book *La Saisiaz* (1878) in a dialogue between Fancy and Reason. In *Asolando*, it has a number of meanings: the contrast between illusion and reality; between what may be desired and what must be accepted; between truth perceived and truth as a deceptive surface; between art and life; between the products of the imagination and the materials upon which they are based; between romanticism and realism. Browning does not favor one over the other. The poems reflect attitudes that swing back and forth between fancy and fact, between a valuing of the imagination and an appreciation of the hard ground of reality.[4]

Although the book contains a representation of the variety of dramatic forms that Browning employed throughout his career, it has a greater number of personal poems than usual. Browning did not often speak with his own voice in his work. We find him present only in his prologues and epilogues and in the opening and closing books of *The Ring and the Book*, which resemble a prologue and epilogue; or he appears very occasionally in a lyric poem like "Oh, to be in England / Now that April's there" or in a poem of statement like "Why I Am a Liberal." Then, in 1887, he published an oblique poetical autobiography, *Parleyings with Certain People of Importance in their Day*, in which he gave glimpses of his intellectual development. *Asolando* takes us again into his personal world. Perhaps in his twilight years Browning was inclined to open his heart more easily.

At the outset, in the "Prologue," he speaks personally in developing the theme of fact and fancy. Browning starts off by having another voice express a common

Romantic attitude about the loss of inspiration that a poet experiences as he grows older. This is an attitude found in Samuel Taylor Coleridge's "Dejection: An Ode" and in Matthew Arnold's "Growing Old," but it is most familiar to us in William Wordsworth's "Ode: Intimations of Immortality from Recollections of Childhood,"[5] which begins,

> There was a time when meadow, grove, and stream.
> The earth, and every common sight,
> > To me did seem
> > Appareled in celestial light,
> The glory and the freshness of a dream.
> It is not now as it hath been of yore;—
> > Turn whereso'er I may,
> > By night or day,
> The things which I have seen I now can see no more.
>
> > The Rainbow comes and goes,
> > And lovely is the Rose,
> > The Moon doth with delight
> Look round her when the heavens are bare,
> > Waters on a starry night
> > Are beautiful and fair;
> The sunshine is a glorious birth;
> But yet I know, where'er I go,
> That there hath passed away a glory from the earth.

The voice that speaks to Browning in the opening lines of the "Prologue" not only expresses a similar sense of loss in intensity of response to the natural world, but it also echoes some of Wordsworth's phrases. "The Poet's age is sad" because in his youth the objects that his eye would see in nature were "At once involved with alien glow— / His own soul's iris-bow." But now "a flower is just a flower: / Man, bird, beast are but beast, bird, man—" no longer surrounded by the coloration of the sort that "when life's day began, / Round each in glory ran."

Browning's reply is a rejection of that reason for regret. He feels that natural objects, just as they are, do not need that fanciful glory—that when objects are seen clearly, they show their true being, their ultimate essence, "truth ablaze, / Not falsehood's fancy-haze." Then he offers, as an example, the way he responded to the beauties of Asolo in his youth, when he felt some of the glow in what he perceived, as compared to what he sees now. Earlier his experience had been like Moses' sight of the Burning Bush, but now "the lambent flame" is gone. "The Bush is bare."

What is the answer to this problem? Another "Voice" now answers—perhaps the Voice of Nature; possibly the Voice of God—and it "straight unlinked / Fancy from Fact," saying that the value of Earth's objects and creatures is there to be apprehended by alert human discernment, "not the eye late dazed": only God can provide transcendence.

This attitude of appreciating reality rather than imagined radiance is frequently found in Browning's work when he shakes off any encumbering romanticism. This view is best known, indeed is best stated, in "Fra Lippo Lippi" (1855) when the painter cries out that he wants to paint reality and show its own simple beauty of being, not some imagined "soul."

> . . . you've seen the world
> —The beauty and the wonder and the power,
> The shapes of things, their colours, lights and shadows,
> Changes, surprises—and God made it all!
> —For what? . . . What's it all about?
> To be passed over, despised? or dwelt upon,
> Wondered at? oh, this last of course!—you say.
> But why not do as well as say,—paint these
> Just as they are, careless of what comes of it?
> God's works—paint any one, and count it crime
> To let a truth slip.

The "Prologue" has been looked on as a Victorian
answer to the Romantic period, but although it does
indeed reply to the ideas and attitudes of Wordsworth's
"Ode," it is greatly inferior as a poem. It offers, it is true,
a defense of the mature eye as it beholds the wonders of
nature, but the resolution of the problem of changing
responses is handled in a mechanical way: suddenly a
"Voice" speaks, cautioning the poet against presuming to
attempt transcendence, against venturing into God's ter-
ritory—which is hardly an "answer." But the chief lim-
itation of the "Prologue," when placed beside Wordsworth's "Ode" is its lack of mellifluous flow. Browning's
knotty, elliptical style here produces no memorable lines
to become embedded in the reader's mental ear. His
very idea, a late-nineteenth-century reversion to realism,
seems to demand expression that is harsher in sound and
more difficult to articulate. Yet Browning's conversational tone and compact statement are appropriate to
what he is saying, and for this volume he has set a thematic conflict that will reverberate throughout its pages.

Another personal poem in *Asolando* harks back to Browning's childhood. In "Development" he again speaks in his own voice but takes a completely different attitude toward the factual. He prefers what his heart tells him this time. He begins to tell a charming story of his childhood interest in Homer's *Iliad*, but he uses it as a parable for a serious theme. What he ultimately expresses is a reliance on his own personal response to reading the Bible and its stories of heroes, prophets, and teachers. He rejects the then recent studies of the biblical texts by German and French scholars who had called into question the commonly held interpretations of the Bible narratives and had pointed out that the Bible was a collection of materials by different hands and from different dates, reassembled by later editors.

A word or two about this nineteenth-century biblical criticism will be helpful at this point. German scholarship, especially at the University of Tübingen had, by study of the dialects of Hebrew, demonstrated that Moses was not the author of the first five books of the Bible but rather they were a patchwork of different narratives and law codes from varying periods and regions. They had also questioned the miracles reported in the Jewish Bible, such as the plagues falling upon Egypt or the opening of the Red Sea. In their New Testament studies they had denied the divinity of Jesus and urged instead that he be regarded as a man who was a great moral teacher and who had suffered crucifixion because of the political and theological conflicts of his time.[6] Such books as *Das Leben Jesu* (1835) by David Strauss (translated into English by George Eliot in 1846), *La Vie de Jesu* (1863) by the French scholar Ernst Renan, and *Essays and Reviews* (1860) by Browning's friend Benjamin Jowett and others—all were widely discussed works with which Browning was thoroughly familiar.[7] In fact, as early as 1850 Browning had published *Christmas-Eve* in which he rejected the rational approach to Jesus's divinity by German scholars in favor of traditional Christian belief. Again, in 1864, in his poem "A Death in the Desert," Browning had created a deathbed monologue of St. John that, in effect, countered the view of Strauss, Renan, and others that the Apostle John could not have been the author of the Fourth Gospel.[8]

But "Development" begins by focusing on Browning's earliest acquaintance with Homer's story of Achilles and the Trojan War. The opening line is a typical example of Browning's conversational blank verse, indeed a real fulfillment of Wordsworth's call for a poetry that would be "the real language of men"[9]: "My father was a scholar and knew Greek."

He tells how his father introduced him, at age five, to the siege of Troy by means of play with the household furniture and the family's dogs and cat. Some years later, seeing that the childhood game had caught the boy's interest, his father recommended a reading of Pope's translation of the *Iliad*. Young Browning, enthralled by the story, was stimulated in his early study of Greek and, after mastering his grammar, was guided by his father to read the *Iliad* in the original with the help of Heine's edition and a dictionary. "I thumbed well and skipped nowise till I learned / Who was who, what was what, from Homer's tongue" to become "The all-accomplished scholar, twelve years old," in full knowledge of the traditional facts about Homer and his supposed authorship not only of the epics of Troy but also the "Battle of the Frogs and Mice" and the Homeric Hymns.

But later his pleasure in his knowledge was disturbed by Homeric criticism, the studies of Friederich Wolf and others: "It's unpleasant work / Their chop and change, *unsettling one's belief*," [my italics]—to discover that the history of Troy was only myth and legend and that Homer was only a name for bards who had passed down the stories by oral tradition to be ordered into a structure by later hands. Yet his heart rebelled against relinquishing something he had cherished.

> No warrant for the fiction, I as fact,
> Had treasured in my heart and soul so long—
> Ay, mark you! and as fact held still, still hold,
> Spite of new knowledge, in my heart of hearts
> And soul of souls, fact's essence freed and fixed
> From accidental fancy's guardian sheath.
>
> . . . .
> . . . ah, Wolf!
> Why must he needs come doubting, spoil a dream?
>
> But then "No dream's worth waking"—Browning says.
> [the original manuscript first read: "Someone says."][10]

"No dream's worth waking" means that "waking" has greater worth than a "dream," but it can also mean (as the whole poem urges), that there is no dream that is worth waking up from. Browning is offering a plea for the importance of art, which has its own reality. But still another ambiguity is involved here: that the Bible is only a fiction too, an implication that Browning here chooses to ignore.

As the poem draws to a close, Browning defends his father's method because it led him to absorb the values upheld in the story of the *Iliad*, "to loathe, like Peleus' son, / A lie as Hell's Gate, love my wedded wife, / Like Hector, and so on with all the rest." He could have learned it out of Aristotle's *Ethics*, but that would have been hard and dull, "'t is a treatise I find hard / To read aright now that my hair is grey / . . . At five years old— how ill had fared its leaves." Better to hold on to the story. Browning cannot let it go and rejects what classical scholarship—and by implication biblical scholarship— tells him.[11]

There a contradiction in the two attitudes that we see in the "Prologue" and "Development." But what we can discern is that Browning will stand up for reality in matters of art and the natural world; yet he will follow his heart in matters of religion and ethics. In some ways he was still a romantic.

In matters of love, especially with regard to his love for Elizabeth, he could be undeniably romantic, and in another personal poem, "Speculative" he has in mind a reunion after death with his wife. This is a brief poem of statement structured in a pair of stanzas that offer two contrasting views of a heavenly condition and a heavenly reward. Neither of them is an especially religious concept. One has a classical view of a "new life in Heaven" with Man, Nature, and Art all renewed. The other is what he himself prays for, a continuation of the reality he knew in his fifteen years of happy marriage.

> Let earth's old life once more enmesh us,
>   You with old pleasure, me—old pain,
> So we but meet nor part again!

Browning said once in a letter to Isa Blagden that reliving that past would be to him pain. She had written him that she was going to Lucca, where he and Elizabeth had spent several happy summers. His response:

> So you go to Lucca. I don't in the least know . . . as to how I should feel on seeing old sights again. The general impression of the past is as if it had been pain. I would not live it over again, not one day of it. Yet all that seems my real *life*,—and before and after, nothing at all: I look back on all my life, when I look *there:* and life is painful. I always think of this when I read the Odyssey—Homer makes the surviving Greeks, whenever they refer to Troy, just say of it "At Troy, where the Greeks suffered so." Yet all their life was in that ten years at Troy. "Lucca, where I suffered so."[12]

But unconscious memory could draw upon that period and find serene happiness too. In "Dubiety," Browning, speaking with the voice of a man in his waning years, records a breath of balm from the past. The season in the poem is autumn, the time of day later afternoon; the wish is to be "happy if but for once / . . . in luxury's sofa-lap of leather"—not settling back for sleep but for comfort. The conditions prevailing are "Outside, / Quiet and peace: inside, nor blame, / Nor want, nor wish whate'er betide." The diction provides a hazy languor for the scene, with terms like "gauziness," "shade," "dim," "dreaming's vapour wreath." Suddenly, a shift occurs in the poem: a sense of déjà vu steals over the speaker, and he relaxes his mind to recapture the mood and identify the occasion. Was it a dream? A vision? No, when called into consciousness, it was a moment in the past "Of what came once when a woman leant / To feel for my brow where her kiss might fall." The final comment, "Truth ever, truth only the excellent!" associates the woman with Elizabeth.[13] But the memory might just as easily be of a mother's kiss.

3

Aspects of Love

ℭ

Poems dealing with love or with the relations between the sexes are scattered throughout *Asolando*, and two of them are among the best from Browning's hand. Throughout his career, he had made outstanding contributions to the poetry of love in English, in lyrics as well as in dramatic poetry: "Meeting at Night," "Parting at Morning," "Love Among the Ruins," "The Last Ride Together," "By the Fireside," and, of course, the brilliant book VI "Caponsacchi," in *The Ring and the Book*. In most of his poems about this area of human activity, he assumes the time-honored Romantic attitude: he asserts that it is important to follow the dictates of the heart, and he thrusts aside reason or the demands of society in favor of love's fulfillment. But Browning is also the realist. He is ready to see love as a powerful human force to be admired and respected and not treated in standard Romantic terms. At times, too, Browning the realist will show us the darker side of human nature as it emerges in problems that men and women have in their love relations.[1]

Browning's Romantic outlook manifests itself in three ways in his poems—and all of them are represented to some extent in *Asolando*. The first of the ways is the simplest and most traditional, reflecting the view that true love is single and intense in its direction, extreme in its expression, and everlasting in its devotion. It is derived from the courtly love tradition of the medieval chivalric romances, wherein the lover holds the beloved as an object of worship for whom he will endure danger, hardship, or humiliation in order to win favor. In this vein, there are four love poems that Browning treats in dramatic form, all of them short, light pieces involving dialogue compressed into the characteristic Browning style.

In "Which?" we have a rhetorical contest, realistic in language but highly romantic in theme, on the definition of love. Three court ladies offer their views about the love they desire from a man; an Abbé is to judge which opinion is best.[2] The Duchesse asks for a man's highest devotion, just below that required for God or for the King. The Marquise goes beyond this, true to the code of chivalric love, asking that the lover perform courageous deeds in battle in her name and that he "Show wounds, each wide mouth to my mercy appealing." A motif of faith and loyalty has been developed so far: the Duchesse sees the lover as faithful to God and loyal to the King, then loving in devotion to her; the Marquise wants her knight's service to exceed "your saint's and your loyalist's praying and kneeling." All this prepares for a folk pattern of three, in which the third lady, the Comtesse, declares that her lover can be both an infidel and a traitor so long as his adoration is for her alone. She wins the judgment, for the Abbé decides without hesitation that this degree of love is most like what God would prefer. In other words, love is a secular form of religion.

The humble position of the lover, a feature of the medieval romances, has been reflected here: the Comtesse's true lover can be a "wretch," a "mere losel," so long as he offers his unswerving love. We find a little of this in "White Witchcraft," a monologue, in which two lovers play a game of imagining each other changed into the form of an animal. The speaker turns his beloved into a fox, "Shy wild sweet stealer of the grapes," but she (named Canidia, the witch in the Roman poet Horace's *Epodes*)[3] turns him into a toad. Still, the tone is playful, and his love survives his degradation: her reply to his acceptance declares that, whether or not he be a fairy-tale toad with a jewel in his brow to denote princely disguise, "his eyes that follow mine—love lasts there, anyhow."

The excess of these Romantic attitudes that have their origin in the literature of chivalry is reached in a confusing poem, "Rosny," in which the speaker, Clara, meditates on her lover, Rosny, who "went galloping into the war." Part of the difficulty lies in the refrain, "Clara, Clara," as line two of each stanza, and "Rosny, Rosny" in the repeated concluding line. Further, the speaker's statement, "Let us two dream" creates as much puzzlement as T. S. Eliot's "Let us go then you and I" in "The Love Song of J. Alfred Prufrock." Is she talking to a friend or to herself?[4] Some of the intruded dialogue in the story is clearly of Clara's imagining, however, in the early part of this four-stanza poem. At first, she supposes that Rosny would suffer a wound, and he is pictured as taking it lightly and asking that his valor be rewarded. Next, Clara is stimulated by the thought of an envious voice of a rival, who scorns mere wounds and asserts that a valiant death is the only true demonstration of love's sacrifice, and she envisions,

> —he lies 'mid a heap
> (Clara, Clara,)
> Of the slain by his hand: what is death but a sleep?
>   Dead, with my portrait displayed on his breast:
> Love wrought his undoing.

If Clara is speaking to a friend, the friend then replies, joining in this irrational demand for sacrifice, "'No prudence could keep / The love-maddened wretch from his fate.'" Clara agrees, "That is best, / Rosny, Rosny." If she is talking to herself, the thoughts are no less romantically absurd.

As often in a dramatic poem of Browning's, his own view of the matter is ambiguous. He is perhaps presenting a criticism of these perverse notions about chivalric love and the extremes to which it may be carried; then, again, he may be swept up in a wave of his own romantic enthusiasm and actually agreeing that the proofs of love should extend even to sacrificial death. I am inclined toward the former interpretation because it is in keeping with his other romantic attitudes about love and more in balance with the realistic views present in other of his love poems. But it is true that Browning seesaws back and forth between a romantic and a realistic outlook throughout his career.

A more down-to-earth love poem, "Poetics" casts scorn on the stock metaphors in praise of a beloved one's beauty. A compact little monologue in two balancing stanzas, it begins with a response to a comment, "So say the foolish!" on the likening of a loved woman to a rose, a swan, a new moon. The speaker chooses instead to value real attributes of his mistress: her sweet breath, her white curved neck, "her human self" far superior to the soft brilliance of the moon.

The next two aspects of Browning's view of Romantic love both have to do with his concept of the "eternal moment."[5] The first of them urges the necessity of true lovers seizing the moment when they perceive their love and acting upon it. This is the situation that precipitates the central action in *The Ring and the Book* (1868). In that book, when Caponsacchi, the priest, comes to the window of Pompilia, the beleaguered heroine, the first words he speaks to her are "I am yours." He then sets out to rescue her. In these narratives of true love, the lovers usually are smitten the first time they see each other. For example, Pompilia's gaze into Caponsacchi's eyes when she looked at him in the theater have a magical effect: he is captivated, and as a result, he undergoes a complete moral transformation.

Browning's poem "By the Fireside" (1855) offers another good illustration. The man and woman in that work have the occasion of joining their souls in love while they walk through the woods. "Oh moment, one and infinite!" states the speaker.

> We two stood there with never a third.
> . . . .
> Oh, the little more, and how much it is!
> And the little less, and what worlds away!
> . . . .
> But we knew that a bar was broken between
> Life and life: we were mixed at last
> In spite of the mortal screen.
> The forests had done it; there they stood;
> We caught for a moment the powers at play:
> They had mingled us so, for once and good.

Conversely, potential lovers who do not seize the moment and act upon their love have a failure in their lives: like the lovers in "The Statue and the Bust" (1855), who delay to run off together, and as a consequence their lives become meaningless.[6]

> The glory dropped from their youth and love,
> And both perceived they had dreamed a dream;
> Which hovered as dreams do, still above:
> But who can take a dream for truth?

Asolando contains two lesser examples of this philosophy of acting on love when the moment is at hand. The first, "Muckle-Mouth Meg," is a comic poem in which fact triumphs over fancy. Browning has composed a jaunty balladlike tale, from a story about the conflicts on the Scottish border.[7] William Scott, "The Lord" (said to be an ancestor of Sir Walter Scott) was captured during his border raid by Gideon Murray, "The Laird," and given a choice of punishments: hanging or marriage to the Laird's ugly daughter. The poem develops the story briskly with quick dialogue exchange in lively Scottish dialect. The young Lord refuses the daughter without even seeing her, ("No mile-wide-mouthed monster of yours do I marry: / Grant rather the gallows!") The Laird's wife, however, grants him a reprieve, choosing to keep him starving in a dungeon to see if he will change his mind.

But Meg, without identifying herself, secretly brings him food every day, and he falls in love with her voice. He tells her, "Did Meg's muckle-mouth boast within some / Such music as yours, mine should match it or burst." A week later, upon release from confinement, he still refuses, and the girl cries "Wow, the obstinate man! / Perhaps he would rather wed me!" When the young Lord agrees and further declares that he would take just her practical wisdom (her "can") for a dowry, she tells him who she is. The poem ends with a vigorous kiss for the bride:

> "Then so—so—so—so—" as he kissed her apace—
> "Will I widen thee out till thou turnest
> From Margaret Minnikin-mou', by God's grace,
> To Muckle-mouth Meg in good earnest!"

The implication is that he will widen her out in more ways than one.

"Inapprehensiveness" presents a situation in which lovers do not act. The woman is imperceptive of the love the man holds for her, and he, on his part, fails to make his timidly held love known to her. The poem is a delicately rendered conversation, like the climactic scene in a Henry James story—and all skillfully handled in run-on couplets. The landscape suggests Asolo, especially as it includes the ruined tower visible from Katharine Bronson's villa, from which foliage had sprung up. As the poem begins, the couple is contemplating the twilight "simply friend-like side by side," when she comments on the beauty of the landscape, especially with the ruin and a shrub branch growing from it contrasted with the hills behind. He replies, asking if Ruskin had written about the picturesqueness of weed growth and ruins, but suddenly he cannot complete his statement for a thought wells up in his mind.

> Oh, fancies that might be, oh, facts that are!
> What of a wilding? By you stands, and may
> So stand unnoticed till the Judgment Day,
> One who, if once aware that your regard
> Claimed what his heart holds,—woke, as from its sward
> The flower, the dormant passion, so to speak—
> Then what a rush of life would startling wreak
> Revenge upon your inapprehensive stare

He is the wilding, there by chance, that could burst into flower if she would only look into his eyes as the sun might and nurture his budding love. But she remains intent upon the distant view and continues the artistic small talk.

>   "No, the book
> Which noticed how the wall-growths wave," said she
> "Was not by Ruskin."
>   I said "Vernon Lee?"

The abrupt ending gives us the inaction of the pair. Neither will venture, although the natural scene has provided the stimulus that had no result. In tone, the poem is not critical of the couple, but rather seems tinged with regret. This poignancy has its origin possibly in the deep-seated feeling that lay within Browning for Katharine Bronson, as Michael Meredith and others have suggested, but was inhibited, I will add, by his being bound lifelong to the wife who was never really dead to him.[8]

The second of the two aspects of Browning's concept of the "eternal moment" involves a mystical or transcendental experience.[9] I use the term *mystical experience* in a rather strict way to refer to a psychological happening that can translate into a person's feeling that one is "going out of oneself" or going beyond time or into some other and unknown realm of life. When religious mystics bring themselves into such a state, they conceive that they have a union with God. St. John of the Cross, engaged in meditation, felt a descent into dark oblivion, which preceded a rise toward illumination and an absence of self in a spiritual oneness with God. The American Protestant mystic, Jonathan Edwards, walking alone in the wilderness suddenly felt a sweetness in the presence of Jesus.

Secular mystics describe a similar psychological process, but they feel instead a oneness with nature or a sense of rising above the universe or of finding themselves in a far-off place. Ralph Waldo Emerson in his book *Nature* describes walking in the woods and suddenly feeling swept up into the spirit of Nature. "I become a transparent eyeball. I am nothing. I see all. The currents of the Universal Being circulate through me. I am part or particle of God."

John Donne in his poem "The Ecstasy" depicts two lovers who, at the moment of sexual union, have their souls go out of themselves and become one soul hovering above them. Like Donne, other poets, philosophers, and saints offer their attempts to describe this psychological experience in terms that suggest sexual climax.

In his brief lyric "Now," Browning manages to convey the embrace of love as a mystical experience, and he employs the paradoxical term "eternal moment" in order to express it. As it develops, the poem stresses aspects of time:

> All of your life that has gone before,
> All to come after it,—so you ignore
> So you make perfect the present,—condense,
> In a rapture of rage, for perfection's endowment,
> Thought and feeling and soul and sense—
> Merged in a moment . . .

There is not only a reduction of vast reaches of time to the flicker of a moment but also the capture of a wholeness of being within that unit of time, followed by an expansion outward beyond immediate space: "You around me for once, you beneath me, above me— / Me . . ." Encapsulated within that time must be a certainty of love: "sure that despite of time future, time past,— / This tick of our life-time 's one moment you love me!" The experience has now transcended the realm of time: "How long such suspension may linger? Ah, Sweet— / The moment eternal—just that and no more." All this is dependent on the physical act of love "When ecstasy's utmost we clutch at the core / While cheeks burn, arms open, eyes shut and lips meet!"

"Now" is an extraordinarily powerful expression of sexual love for the poet to have composed in the last years of his life. After a lifetime of concern about his privacy and in an age that discouraged revelation of sexual feeling, Browning, at the end of his career, has furnished a suggestion of his capacity for sexual intensity, the secret, no doubt, of his ability to write so many poems about love during half a century.[10]

One more poem in *Asolando* uses the same idea of the eternal moment. A short piece based upon the lore of the *Arabian Nights*, "A Pearl, A Girl," begins with the description of a pearl ring with a magic property: to that stone one can "Whisper the right word" and "lo, you are lord . . . / Of heaven and earth." This is all a metaphor for the power within a woman: "Utter the true word," the word of love, and she "escapes her soul," like the genie within the pearl:

> I am wrapt in blaze,
> Creation's lord, of heaven and earth
> Lord whole and sole—by a minute's birth—
> Through the love in a girl!

But Browning is not always the romantic. In some of his work he displays a realistic awareness of the problems that love can create. He knows that the course of love can go wrong with mismatched people or that difficulties can arise in any intimate and passionate relationship between the sexes. Poems of this sort had continued to crop up in Browning's earlier work, such items as "Any Wife to Any Husband," "A Woman's Last Word," "Andrea del Sarto," "The Lost Mistress." In *Asolando*, the amusing poem "Humility," is not really on the darker side of love, but it moves away from romantic idealism. It begins by developing the metaphorical example of a girl who gathers an armload of flowers, drops a bud on the way home, but, having so many, does not pick it up. With this as his parable, the worldly-wise speaker urges women to give a lover an abundance of love, to make him thus wealthy; then when—"stealthy / Work it was!"—he picks up what love might fall to him, it would not be missed—nor would he be poor in what he gets: "Not the worst bud—who can tell?"

In its exploration of a troubled marriage, the sequence of four poems, "Bad Dreams," is reminiscent of Browning's "James Lee's Wife" (1864), although both the man and the woman speak in the poems. However, this literary attempt to plunge into the psyche is not successful, for the sequence is not really coherent.[11] There is very little except the dreaming to provide any linkage between one poem and another. The chief interest for a reader is to see Browning's handling of nightmare materials and to see that he recognized that "Sleep leaves a door on hinge / Whence soul, ere our flesh suspect, / Is off and away."[12] "Bad Dreams I" is very brief, conveying to us the wife's dream of her husband's infidelities, but she wakes to find she still loves him. "Bad Dreams II" shows the husband's dream of estrangement in marriage as depicted by dancing couples, "Each grasped each, past escape / In a whirl or weary or worse: / Man's sneer met woman's curse." Although some commentators have seen a likeness in the sequence to George Meredith's *Modern Love*,[13] there is actually a closer resemblance to the surrealistic visions of James Thomson's *City of Dreadful Night*. The husband's dream includes a Gothic scene of a chapel where "a low lamp burned," a demonic figure sits enthroned, and the wife enters to kneel before him as the dreamer says "I decline / To tell—what I saw, in fine!" This irrational husband's accusatory dream is depicted by Browning in lurid melodramatic language: "Expurgate . . . your soul of its ugly stain" and "ah, what ensued / From draughts of a drink hell-brewed?" When he tells his wife the dream, she counters lightheartedly with a dream of her own in which she had to pass an examination about *The Greek Anthology* and had said, in one answer, that Hannah More (an eighteenth-century social reformer and writer of religious tracts) had translated a licentious epigram from the Greek. The ending of the poem is so abrupt as to seem frivolous.

"Bad Dreams III" gives another nightmarish scene to the husband, this time of a primeval forest invading "a lucid City / Of architectural device / Every way perfect." The City and the Forest devour each other, representing Art and Nature in mortal conflict. If the dream is to be related to the problems of the husband and wife, it would seem to suggest that Freud's *Civilization and Its Discontents* is being enacted: natural impulses repressed by society's demands take their revenge but in turn are choked: "pavements, as with teeth, / Griped huge weed widening crack and split / In squares. . . ." "Bad Dreams III" is the most successful poem in the sequence.

"Bad Dreams IV" finds the wife's nightmare of her gravestone visited by "My life's cold critic bent on blame /

Of all poor I could do or say." But the husband dissolves into tears crying "Only be as you were! Abound / In foibles, faults,—laugh, robed and crowned / As Folly's veriest queen—care I / One feather-fluff? Look pity, Love, / On prostrate me." She sees then he is looking at the date inscribed in the stone, "when one chance stab/ Of scorn . . ." (the statement goes no further but implies the words would have continued as something like "devastated my heart.") The dream makes clear that the wife felt overcome by verbal abuse and criticism but imagines a repentant husband. No good future is augured in this bleak marriage.[14]

I prefer to end the chapter with a more positive consideration of love. "Summum Bonum" is like in spirit to "Now"; both are brief lyrics in which the "I" is a *persona* through which the poet offers an exquisite expression of feeling in order to transfer it to the reader to share. "Summum Bonum" is a one-sentence lyric outburst that deals with epitomes and essences. Distillation of three of the areas of the natural world are depicted: the sweetness of the world of growing things, the riches of the mineral earth, and the beauty of all sea life.

> All the breath and the bloom of the year in the bag of
>   one bee:
> All the wonder and wealth of the mine in the heart of
>   one gem:
> In the core of one pearl all the shade and the shine
>   of the sea

These alliterating nouns are given further patterns of repetition as the statement moves to include virtues,

Truth and Trust, that stand above and beyond the natural world. All these essences are discovered as condensed—"In the kiss of one girl."

The intensity of the physical experience of love had not been forgotten by the seventy-seven-year-old poet.

4

Art as Perspective

The poems relating to the arts in *Asolando* are not as memorable as Browning's great dramatic monologues about Italian painters and musicians; yet they are all worthwhile compositions, and they reflect some of Browning's most characteristic ideas about the quality and function of art.

The first of these ideas is a Platonic one, namely, that the response to physical beauty leads to a perception of beauty of soul. Plato presents this idea in his dialogue *The Symposium*, in which Socrates and others discourse on the beautiful and try to define it. Browning's best known offering of this idea was put into the mouth of Fra Lippo Lippi in 1855 when the friar-painter described the conflict with his Prior, who had ordered his realistic fresco to be destroyed because it depicted the human body in its natural likeness and did not represent what the Prior called "soul." Lippi replied,

> Why can't a painter lift each foot in turn,
> Left foot and right foot, go a double step,
> Make his flesh liker and his soul more like,
> Both in their order? Take the prettiest face,
> The Prior's niece . . . patron saint—is it so pretty

You can't discover if it means hope, fear,
Sorrow or joy? Won't beauty go with these?
Suppose I've made her eyes all right and blue,
Can't I take breath and try to add life's flash,
And then add soul and heighten them threefold?
Or say there's beauty with no soul at all—
(I never saw it—put the case the same—)
If you get simple beauty and naught else,
You get about the best thing God invents:
That's somewhat: and you'll find the soul you have missed,
Within yourself. . . .

Since Robert Browning idealized women, he thought that painting a woman's body realistically was a way to reflect that inner femaleness that he admired most. In 1887, in his poem "Parleying with Francis Furini," he developed a full treatment of this idea, focusing on the career of a painter who painted female nudes. In the poem, Browning refuses to believe a story about Furini on his deathbed. It seems that Filippo Baldinucci, in his *Notizie de' Professori del Designo* (1681–1728), told an anecdote about Furini, who was both a priest and a painter, that when he was dying he asked his friends to burn all the paintings of nudes that he had created in his life: he feared that God would punish him, the priest, for looking at the nude bodies of his models.[1] Browning rejects this story as a fabrication because he knew that Baldinucci disapproved of the nude in painting, thought it was obscene. In the poem, Browning pays tribute to "God's best of beauteous and magnificent / Revealed to earth— the naked female form."

He tells Furini to pray to God thanking him for his

ability as a painter to perceive the beauty of the human body:

> Bounteous God,
> Deviser and Dispenser of all gifts
> To soul through sense,—in Art the soul uplifts
> Man's best of thanks! What but Thy measuring-rod
> Meted forth heaven and earth? more intimate,
> Thy very hands were busied with the task
> Of making, in this human shape a mask
> A match for that divine. . . .
> some few
> Have grace to see Thy purpose, strength to mar
> Thy work by no admixture of their own,
> —Limn truth not falsehood, bid us love alone
> The type untampered with, the naked star![2]

These are the ideas behind the poem, "The Lady and the Painter," a dialogue in tetrameter lines arranged in four stanzas so skillfully rhymed that the dialogue flows freely beyond the rhymed line-endings. The poem is dramatic in more than form, for it presents a clear conflict of ideas developed in a structure of three parts: Lady Blanche's accusation of the painter, the painter's digression about the feathers in Lady Blanche's hat, and his application of the digression to her.

The poem begins in good Browning fashion in the middle of a conversation, as Lady Blanche objects to the painter's practice of painting nudes, by using unclothed female models:

> To help Art-study,—for some dole
> Of certain wretched shillings—you

> Induce a woman—virgin too—
> To strip stark naked?

The painter's rhyming answer, "True,"[3] is followed by his asking her what the decorations are on her hat. When she tells him that they are the feathers of wild birds and that the Parisian fashion will extend itself to feathered dresses next season, he tells her that he would feel less disgust

> Did you strip off those spoils you wear,
> And stand—for thanks, not shillings—bare,
> To help Art like my Model there.

The model has received praise from the painter (like Browning's for Francis Furini)

> for God's surpassing good,
> Who granted to my reverent gaze
> A type of purest womanhood,

and the painter challenges Lady Blanche "clothed with murder" of God's "harmless beings" to match his model's behavior. The poem ends ironically as Lady Blanche does not understand, or pretends not to understand, him and replies that he is joking.

The subtheme of the poem is congruent with Browning's longstanding support of the antivivisection cause as a social issue during Victorian times. As a tribute recognizing his help, the Society for the Prevention of Vivisection sent a huge floral wreath to Westminster Abbey for Browning's funeral.[4]

Another poem "Beatrice Signorini" takes its rise directly from Baldinucci's book and tells the story of Francesco Romanelli and his attraction to Artemesia Gentileschi, the most celebrated woman painter of the Italian Renaissance. The work is in pentameter couplets. Although couplets, because of their sense of closure every two lines, tend to make choppy progress, Browning handles them adroitly as run-on couplets, thus giving his narrative and dialogue a flow. This is a skill he had been displaying all his career, ever since "My Last Duchess" back in 1842.

The poem, strictly speaking, is not a dramatic narrative, for Browning as narrator speaks in his own voice, not assuming a role of any sort. But in his treatment, the work does bear a resemblance to his dramatic monologues, for his focus on Romanelli offers an ironical view: the painter's own thoughts reveal him to be a pompous fool. At the same time, Browning never allows us to see into the mind of Artemesia, whose statements and actions remain ambiguous.

Romanelli's inadequacy as a painter leads us to another concept about art that Browning held. He assumed the Romantic idea that imperfection in artistic products revealed the soul of the artist, and as a consequence, works with imperfections were more aesthetically valuable than works that had no flaws. This view, subscribed to by several Victorians, seems to have developed as a reaction to the rise of industrialism and the factory system: machines could turn out perfect products, but what is natural will be imperfect, therefore, have greater value.[5]

Browning's best-known presentation of this idea had appeared in "Andrea del Sarto" (1855), subtitled ironically "The Faultless Painter"—Andrea is thus inferior to Raphael, Michelangelo, and Leonardo da Vinci, and he knows it. As he explains to his wife in the poem:

> I do what many dream of, all their lives,
> —Dream? strive to do, and agonize to do,
> And fail in doing. I could count twenty such
> On twice your fingers, and not leave this town . . .
> Yet do much less, so much less . . .
> Well, less is more, Lucrezia. I am judged.
> There burns a truer light of God in them.
> In their vexed beating stuffed and stopped-up brain,
> Heart, or whate'er else, than goes on to prompt
> This low-pulsed forthright craftsman's hand of mine.

In the poem, he has a copy of a Raphael panel in his studio. He recognizes that the arm of one of the figures is not correctly painted. But when he takes a piece of chalk to show how the arm can be rendered properly, the painting loses its quality of greatness.

"Beatrice Signorini," a work of some length and complexity, was Browning's favorite poem in *Asolando*. It intertwines three narrative elements: the revelation of Romanelli as an inferior artist both in his work and in his moral being; the characterization of Artemesia, the woman he is attracted to, as a superior artist and a perceptive person; and the triumph of Romanelli's wife, Beatricé Signorini, in asserting herself and changing her husband's behavior.[6]

Browning begins to recount the story as a comedy of art history in language of colloquial ease, introducing Romanelli of Viterbo as a mediocre painter, calling him

FIG. 12. "L'Inclinazione" ("Desire") by Artemesia Gentileschi, Casa Buonarroti, Florence. Photo, Richard Kennedy. Baldinucci, shocked by the nudity, later caused the figure to be draped.

"greatish-small," "Cortona's drudge," and stating "whether he spoiled fresco more or less, / And what 's its fortune, scarce repays your guess." But Browning, a forgiving man, is willing to overlook his faults because of one circumstance and urges the reader to do likewise. Hence our story.

We learn that when Romanelli went to Rome, he came to know Artemesia Gentileschi, who was in the full course of a brilliant career and who, as creator of a great nude entitled "Desire," horrified Baldinucci. ("Hang his book and him," is Browning's dismissal.) Romanelli develops a passion to possess Artemesia and even her genius, "what we term / The very self, the God-gift whence had grown / Heart's life and soul's life,—how make that his own?" Yet he blindly thinks himself "the abler-skilled" in art. ("So he conceited:" Browning interjects, "mediocrity / Turns on itself the self-transforming eye.") But now we discover that Romanelli is married, and we learn something about his domestic situation: that his wife thinks he is a great painter and that she allows and forgives him his philandering. Romanelli is patronizingly appreciative, "Good Beatricé Signorini! Well / And wisely did I choose her."

In his campaign to win Artemesia, he considers submitting himself to her superiority, for he regards true love as the joining of two souls in which "one must bend, one rule above." But his male pride rejects this position; anyone who would do that would be "half woman not whole man." Man must be master.[7]

As he is considering his approach to Artemesia, we find that he is a perfectionist in art, like Andrea del

Sarto. He thinks to coach her in her drawing, "If the acromion had a deeper dint, / That shoulder were perfection." We also learn more about his philosophy of living, that although married he still claims the male privilege to wander, "I may drink / At many waters, must repose by none— / Rather arise and fare forth. . . . Best depart / From this last lady I have learned by heart!" And having so decided that he has a man's right to pursue Artemesia, he need not conceal his actions from Beatricé who would be easily pacified:

> and should a stray tear steal
> From out the blue eye, stain the rose cheek—bah!
> A smile, a word 's gay reassurance—ah,
> With kissing interspersed,—shall make amends,
> Turn pain to pleasure.

An abrupt jump in scene occurs, not an unusual occurrence in Browning's work. We intrude into the middle of a dialogue with Artemesia the next day that reveals she is breaking off her professional relationship with Romanelli and sending him back to Viterbo and his wife. She is also making his wife a gift of a painting, a border of flowers around an empty space. Romanelli himself must paint a human face in the middle, "her whom you like best!" She explains, giving perhaps a hint that she has been attracted to him as well, that his art

> shall wed
> My own, be witness of the life we led
> When sometimes it has seemed our souls near found
> Each one the other as its mate—unbound

Had yours been haply from the better choice
—Beautiful Bicé . . .

And perhaps there is even a suggestion that she would like herself to be the center of the picture:

Make whom you like best
Queen of the central space, and manifest
Your predilection for what flower beyond
All flowers finds favour with you. I am fond
Of—say—yon rose's rich predominance,
While you—what wonder?—more affect the glance
The gentler violet from its leafy screen
Ventures—so choose your flower and paint your queen!

Romanelli with headlong decision seizes his brushes and paints the portrait of Artemesia herself into the flower-wreathed center. When he returns home to his wife, he unloads a chest of jewels, medals, and gold chains— "gifts of Prince and Bishop, Church and State," which please Beatricé. He thinks scornfully of her response to these "toys /—Trinkets and trash," wondering what more worthwhile things would touch the depths of Artemesia. Then, as a test, he declares he had yet to disclose the most valuable gift of all. He unveils the portrait of Artemesia surrounded by flowers and, with unpardonable insensitivity, cries "Be sincere! / Say, should you search creation far and wide, / Was ever a face like this?"

Beatricé now turns art critic, commenting judiciously on each of the flowers until suddenly she whips the long pin out of her hair to stab and slash the face out of the canvas. Then casting away her destructive instrument, with folded arms "Bicé stood / Passively statuesque, in quietude/ Awaiting judgment."

Romanelli's response, and this is why Browning forgives him, is loud, appreciative laughter and joyous praise at seeing his wife take fire: she is

> no occulted star
> But my resplendent Bicé, sun-revealed,
> Full-rondure! Woman-glory unconcealed,
> So front me, find and claim and take your own—
> My soul and body yours and yours alone,
> As you are mine, mine wholly!

So our comedy has its happy ending, and Browning relents, somewhat, in his judgment of Romanelli's painting, although his language betrays that his opinion has changed very little ("And I fain would hope—some say / Indeed for certain—that our painter's toils / At fresco-splashing, finer stroke in oils, / Were not so mediocre after all.") Even his words of praise hint at Romanelli's place among the "faultless" painters: "He designed / Correctly, nor in colour lagged behind / His age."

The poem has been a great success in its method of comic characterization and its pricking of self-aggrandizement and sexual pride. But in its treatment of the enigmatic Artemesia, it has another element contributing to complexity. In jumping from Romanelli's schemes of possessing Artemesia to their conversation in parting the next day, Browning has left open the reader's understanding of what their relationship had been. Had Romanelli made his advances? And because of his prideful blunder-

ing, is she gracefully and teasingly breaking off their association? "I'll divorce / Husband and wife no longer," she
declares as her reason, offering special considerate praise
for Beatricé as that "paragon" that Romanelli has chosen
among the beauteous women of Viterbo.

Artemesia's reasons for the gift are likewise ambiguous. The painting is for Beatricé. Is she, out of sisterly
solidarity, inviting the bumbling husband to create a
tribute for his wife? But the gift also poses a test for
Romanelli. Do her words about wedding their art together and their nearly finding that they were soul mates
offer a temptation for him to add her portrait to the
flower frame and thus create a problem for him at home?
Is she wanting to punish him for his presumption in
reaching for her? The choice of flowers as a wreathe
around the space has allowed Browning to include a long
digression about the symbolic significance of flowers for
lovers. This prods the reader to look carefully at Artemesia's words about roses and violets. Is she deliberately
provoking his male assertiveness into choosing the rose
rather than being satisfied with the gentle violet? Or
would she really find pleasure in having him choose her
as the center of the picture?

These are the kinds of questions that Browning's best
dramatic poems can put forward. In giving his opinion
that "Beatrice Signorini" was the best poem in *Asolando*,
Browning was showing his preference for the inconclu-
sive, the uncertain, the ambiguous in poetry. With a
poem like this, the reader must enter Browning's imagined world, weigh the problems of judgment, and feel all
the emotional and intellectual conflicts they entail.[8]

FIG. 13. The Angel at the Ponte dell' Angelo, Venice.
Courtesy Rosella Mamoli Zorzi.

"Ponte dell' Angelo, Venice" a comic poem in the form of a dramatic narrative, likewise deals with historical anecdote, but it is a simple, clearly developed legend set in Venice. Browning's language is even more colloquial here, with tumbling syntax including parenthetical intrusions and hasty additions, even though the poem is composed in rhymed stanzas, whose tetrameter lines move fast.

> Stop rowing! This one of our bye-canals
> O'er a certain bridge you have to cross
> That's named "Of the Angel": listen why!
> The name "Of the Devil" too much appals
> Venetian acquaintance, so—his the loss
> While the gain goes . . . look on high!

And the speaker points to the angel carved over the coat of arms on a Venetian house. Thence the tale ostensibly accounts for the presence of that angel, but a heavy charge of criticism is fired at lawyers on the way.

The story is told of a Venetian attorney who is so greedy for gain that he squeezes all his clients, even the poor ones. His one redeeming virtue (Browning usually looks to forgive) is his nightly prayer to the Virgin for her protection. At the end of one particularly profitable week, when he had made money out of a poor widow, even though he had lost her case, the lawyer decided that he needed to fumigate his house, morally speaking, by inviting a holy man to dine, the Head of the Capuchins. When the monk sees that the lawyer's serving man is a specially trained ape, he suspects the presence of a demon and calls out words of exorcism. Lo, Satan appears and, in a dialogue with the monk, explains that he lies in wait for the lawyer to neglect his nightly prayer because only then can he seize him for his sins and carry him off. After further exorcising words from the monk, Satan makes a hasty departure, causing a rent in the wall.

> Wide bat-wings, spread arms and legs, tail out a-stream,
> Crash obstacles went, right and left, as he soared
> Or else sank, was gone clean through the hole anyhow.

The monk's second miracle, wringing blood from a napkin, proves to the lawyer the extent of his sins: this is the blood squeezed from his poor clients. Such a sight sends the lawyer to his knees in repentance, vowing restitution. The monk in a final act of mercy advises patching the hole in the wall with the effigy of an angel, to prevent the demon's return. With this explanation for the presence of the angel carved on the house, we are back to the scene in the gondola. In conclusion, Browning points in mock-serious manner to the authority for his tale

> All's down in a book.
> Gainsay me? Consult it! Still faithless? Trust *me*?
> Trust Father Boverio[9] who gave me the case
> In his Annals . . .

The last comic touch is a defense of tradition rather than fact:

> And thereby we learn—would we ascertain truth—
> To trust wise tradition, which took, at the time,
> Note that served till slow history ventured on fact,
> Though folk have their fling at tradition forsooth!

"Flute-Music, with an Accompaniment" moves into another realm of art—music. It takes up the principal theme that our book has been playing with: the contrast between illusion and reality, between something imagined and something factual—again in a dialogue, which is the "accompaniment" to the flute music. This material is arranged in a pattern of stanzas in trimeter lines with every third line of a quatrain in tetrameter. The short lines are suitable to the flute music and in addition Browning supplies frequent alliterating phrases appropriate to rhythmical flute notes—for example,

> Bullfinch-bubblings, soft sounds suiting
>   What sweet thoughts, I wonder?
> Fine-pearled notes that surely
>   Gather dewdrop-fashion,
> Deep-down in some heart which purely
>   Secretes globuled passion—

The dialogue takes place between two lovers, an intellectual exchange, in which the man's deep response to the flute music that he hears floating over the ashtree tops is opposed by the woman's pejorative comments, which result from her having heard the music played many times. In the course of the discussion, he turns to an analogy between the flute playing and love, and the tremulous relationship between the man and the woman becomes the center of attention. One of Browning's firmly held ideas about music emerges early in the poem as the young man, hearing the flute music, wonders what the flute music is telling him and suggests that it is speaking about love. Browning, who was himself very musical (he played the piano and the organ; he loved to attend concerts), judged that music was supreme among the arts, that it could express emotion, interior feeling, beyond what painting could do visually or poetry could say in words. As the young man listens, he hears the flute music treat of the various aspects of love, "Assurance— / Trust—entire Contentment / —Passion proved by much endurance," Sorrow, Hope, Joy, calm Acquiescence. C. Castan in an illuminating article[10] points out that the music Browning chose to have the flautist play is "Ah! lève-toi, soleil" from act 2, scene 2, of Gounod's *Romeo et Juliette*, an aria from the "waking scene" after the wedding night and thus very suitable for the speaker in the poem to interpret in the way he does.

His musing is interrupted by the woman: "All's your fancy-spinning!" She tells him that the flute player is a neighbor, an accountant, who practices ("Never-ending, still beginning") during his lunch hour, working with an instruction book that takes him from the easy pieces through the more difficult and that he plays very poorly, "Till as lief I'd hear some Zulu's / Bone-piped bag"— listen to the way he handles that *legato*, his fingers making it *staccato*. There is even a hint, as the poem goes on, that she knows the flute player and that he has rejected her love some time in the past.[11]

The young man replies that music needs a listener and he has supplied that part, even though he did not know that it was only the flute player practicing pieces she had heard him try many times. He chides her for being over-critical because of the many repetitions, that she would "Find stale thrush-songs tiresome" and prefer some

"Owl's fresh hooting." Her answer comes, that a practiced ear develops taste and judgment; whereas he has only heard the flute player once and, what is more, has heard his faults muffled by or filtered through the ashtree tops.

The dialogue now takes a crucial turn as the poem moves into its final section. The young man points an analogy between her listening to the flute playing and her response to love. He wonders if her words suggest an attitude she has expressed toward him, that the shy, stumbling words of a lover are to her only "Tricks tried— oh, so often!—" to ensnare a heart. As a counter to this, he offers a complex sequence of metaphors. The beauty of a briar rose droops at midday and the frosty glow of a hedge-sloe becomes clouded by road-dust; yet, sprinkle them with water and their freshness is restored. Like the water, distance through the treetops brightens the music; distance created through shy behavior softens the peevishness or other irritating traits of the beloved; distance created by a day's absence deflects a critical eye.

> Bear but one day's exile,
> Ugly traits were wholly lost or
> Screened by fancies flexile—

Thus "Fancies' interference / Changed . . ."—he was about to say "my view of your faults," but he does not complete the statement. Instead, he continues his defence of fancies:

> But since I sleep, don't wake me!
> What if all 's appearance?
> Is not outside seeming

> Real as substance inside?
> Both are facts, so leave me dreaming:
> If who loses wins I'd
> Ever lose . . .

He sounds like Andrea del Sarto recognizing that less is more. The end of the discussion seems to warn that it is dangerous to interfere with his indulgence in fancies, whether about flute music or about love.

"Flute-Music, with an Accompaniment" is a subtly developed poem, full of nuances, suggested perhaps by Browning's view that music can convey meaning more fully and deeply than words are able to do. He thus has his young man try to reach beyond language, both to interpret the flute music and to describe the winding ways of love, and in so doing Browning gives him partial statements, images, hints, ambiguous musings, and a broken-off sentence. All this is counterpointed by the woman's blunt, cynical remarks, which may be attempts to conceal rather than reveal. The result is a tantalizingly complex work.[12]

Questions of fact and fancy are very slippery. The hard fact of painting from nude models should not give way before fancies about the artist's attitude toward the women who pose for him. Fancies about male superiority vanish when confronted by the presence of wise or self-assured females. Tradition is inclined to fancifulness when the hard facts of history are absent. Fancies lend a power to a music lover's ear but also provide a protective shield from the inevitable uncertainties and misunderstandings in matters of love.

5

Religion and Power

As he does in most of his collections of poems, Browning includes in *Asolando* several poems on religious subjects or on figures associated historically with the Church. Three of them deal with popes and cardinals. But before turning to them we should first remind ourselves of his religious background. Robert Browning was brought up as a Congregationalist.[1] Since he and his parents did not belong to the Church of England, they were classified as Dissenters. They were Chapel, not Church. They lived on the south side of the Thames River where most of the Nonconformist families of London were clustered. Being Dissenters, the Brownings were to some degree outsiders. Robert could not attend Oxford or Cambridge because the universities accepted only members of the Church of England; he had to enroll at the newly established University of London. Although there was a strong tradition of anti-Catholicism in England because of the religious conflicts of the fifteenth and sixteenth centuries, the dissenting sects, being descendants of the Puritans, were even more opposed to the Church of Rome than the Anglicans were.

But Robert's mother was a mild woman in her social

attitudes and his father was a very broad-minded man with wide literary and cultural interests. There was an atmosphere of religious tolerance in the Browning home.[2] In fact, when Robert was a young man, he spent a great deal of time with Unitarian families and developed a universalist tendency in his beliefs—that is, he seems to have believed that God in his infinite mercy would not condemn human beings to eternal damnation, that eventually everyone would find salvation. When he married Elizabeth Barrett in the 1840s, he was drawn back more closely to Congregationalism because Elizabeth was also a Nonconformist and was devoutly religious. It was for her that he wrote the long poem *Christmas-Eve*, which shows his religious beliefs more clearly than in any other work.

In *Christmas-Eve*, the speaker in the poem, tired and disgusted with the services at a Congregational Chapel, falls asleep and has a dream of a visit to St. Peter's in Rome during a Christmas Eve Mass and later to a German lecture hall, where the professor is discussing biblical myths. But the speaker is dissatisfied with the overly elaborate ceremony at the Mass and even more with the dry rationalism of the German university. He returns to the Chapel congregation and concludes ultimately that he has found his true religious home with these humble worshippers and their simple religious fundamentals.

It is, then, as an undogmatic Protestant Christian that Browning lived his religious life in the Victorian era. During the time he and Elizabeth lived in Italy, however, he became more fully acquainted with the Roman Catholic Church and sometimes even attended Mass at the great cathedrals. In this way, he came to appreciate the art and culture of the Church more fully than he had before. He was aware that saints and leaders of the Church and hordes of humble believers led admirable lives and were worthy of respect as honest, faithful Christians.[3] His characterization of the Pope in *The Ring and the Book* stands as the philosophical high point of that book, and the character of Pompilia is developed as that of a true saint who converts Caponsacchi back to his religious duties and seems possibly to have wrought a miraculous change in Guido at the very end.[4]

But he also recognized that most of the officials of the Roman Church were more worldly than the leaders of the dissenting sects in England. Thus in his poems they were satirized or treated with a light, comic touch. The three poems in *Asolando* about cardinals and popes are all mildly comic.

The first, "The Cardinal and the Dog," is the only poem in the book that was written early. Browning composed it in 1841 and a year later copied it out to amuse William Macready's son, "Willie," when the boy was ill, so that he could draw illustrations for it (just as he had done for Browning's "The Pied Piper of Hamlin.") The poem versifies a legend about Cardinal Crecenzio, who supposedly had a fearful vision of a huge black dog that haunted him until he fell into a decline and died. In medieval tradition, a black man or a black dog was often an emissary of Satan charged to carry off a sinner to hell. Cardinal Crecenzio, a papal legate who had presided over five sessions of the Council of Trent, had been very tough-minded in his opposition to Protestantism and

Church reform. Indeed, the Council was a powerful force of the Counter-Reformation. Thus, the legend was probably of Protestant origin.[5]

With this as his subject, Browning produced a comic poem, even though it told about a man who was frightened to death. He used a seven-stress line that breaks in the middle to resemble ballad stanzas of four-stress and three-stress lines alternating, a pattern that contributes to lightness of tone. His phrasing and rhythm often create comic effects—for instance, his using all of line two to record the date, except for the last word, which is tacked on to form an amusing rhyme: "Crecenzio, the Pope's Legate at the High Council, Trent, / —Year Fifteen hundred twenty-two, March Twenty-five—intent. . . ." The final touch in the poem is a joking conclusion (reflecting a characteristic Browning mildness about death and judgment) after the death of the Cardinal: "Heaven keep us Protestants from harm: the rest . . ."; Browning throws in an ellipsis for a pause, as if he were going to suggest "can go to the devil," but then gives a surprise reprieve to finish his rhyme, "no ill betide!"

The next poem, "The Pope and the Net," is a comic dramatic anecdote, again in that seven-stress line but this time rhyming in triplets, about a fictitious pope who had made use of his lowly beginnings to impress the College of Cardinals with his humility.[6] The speaker is a gossipy cardinal who utters a cry of surprise in the opening lines, "What, he on whom our voices unanimously ran, / Made Pope at out last Conclave?" We then get the exposition of what provoked his outburst. As a child, this new pope had helped his father, a fisherman, with his work. He had risen in the Church from deacon, to priest, to bishop, to cardinal. When he became a cardinal, there was some sniggering among his peers about his humble start in life—says one, "Saint Peter's net, instead / Of sword and keys, is come in vogue!" But the newly chosen cardinal made a show of his origins by hanging a fisherman's net in his palace hall, declaring that it was his way of reminding himself that he should exhibit no pride in his rise and be humble. This practice so strikes his colleagues as evidence of his saintly humility that eventually they elect him Pope.

Browning now proceeds to an enactment of the cardinals kissing the Pope's slipper (a ceremony that Protestants find an absurd obeisance) on which occasion they discover that the fishing net no longer hangs on the wall. When a spokesman queries the Pope about it, he gets the reply, "Son, it hath caught the fish," a display of wit and wiliness that leaves us regarding the new Pope as a likeable con man.

Browning's third poem on the actions of high dignitaries of the Church, "The Bean-Feast," is based on a true happening in the life of Pope Sixtus V, who, Browning informs us, was indeed the son of a swineherd. Again, he uses that seven-beat line, but the fact that he moves the caesura back and forth, not providing those regular breaks after the fourth stress, indicates that this is a more seriously developed characterization. The story, told as a straight narrative in Browning's own voice, is about the practice Sixtus had of going about Rome in disguise to inquire into the welfare of his people.

One night, when he came upon a family in a miserable

hovel, he set about "to learn how lowliest subjects bore hunger, toil, and cold." Man, wife, and children were enjoying a simple repast of beans. When the Pope intruded to ask "Are times good, masters gentle? Your grievances unlock! / How of your work and wages?— pleasures, if such may be— / Pains, as such are for certain." But since the people are suspicious of this prying stranger, the Pope reveals himself and is then welcomed as an honor to their dwelling. When he joins them in a plate of beans, he seems to recall his own rise to power from earthy beginnings and to become aware of God's continued presence in the most basic functions of daily life: "Thy goodness nowise scants / Man's body of its comfort,—that I whom kings and queens / Crouch to, pick crumbs from off my table, relish beans!" The poem concludes with his thankful prayer for God's simplest benefits—appetite and digestion.

The figures of power in the Roman Catholic hierarchy whom Browning characterizes are, indeed, seen from a Protestant perspective. But his attitude toward them varies, depending on the historical character whose life is being examined. A Catholic foe of the Reformation is seen as vulnerable to God's judgment. A schemer whose position results from calculated appearances rather than actual virtues is depicted as a political rather than a religious Prince of the Church. But a holder of the highest rank, if his intentions be good and his pride be in abeyance, is honored as worthy of office and appreciated as a responsible leader.

Students today regard Browning's "Rephan" as his one venture into science fiction. This poem is a fantasy about a person who was born on another planet, Rephan,[7] but was dissatisfied with its perfection and so came to planet Earth. It displays that same Romantic valuation of imperfection that crops up in Browning's poems about art, except that this time his idea does not just apply to painting but criticizes the desire for perfection in the whole of life. We might call the poem an anti-Utopian romance.

The speaker seems to be a woman—indeed she echoes the voice of the Statue of Liberty in Emma Lazarus's poem[8] when, in her motherly way, she calls the troubled children of Earth to gather round:

> Let my circle embrace your worn, your weak,
> Brow-furrowed old age, youth's hollow cheek—
> Diseased in the body, sick in soul,
> Pinched poverty, satiate wealth,—your whole
> Array of despairs! Have I read the roll?

She asks that her hearers let imagination loose here in order to understand what life on Rephan was like:

> Let drift the helm,
> Let drive the sail, dare unconfined
> Embark for the vastitude, O Mind,
> Of an absolute bliss!

She describes a world like Plato's spiritual realm of Ideas where there is "nowhere deficiency nor excess," no want, no fear, no pain, no growth, no hope, no change, a timeless world of continuous happiness where each person is self-fulfilled, thus needing no relationship with fellow creatures.

The question arises, when did she become restive in

that realm of perfection? Did God plant the seed of discontent? No matter. "I yearned for no sameness but difference." Thus she was able to conceive of "an Infinite / Discovered above and below me." As a consequence, she could experience the strivings of imperfection, similar to what Andrea del Sarto recognized.

> Oh, gain were indeed to see above
> Supremacy ever—to move, remove
> Not reach—aspire yet never attain
> To the object aimed at!

Even suffering was an experience to be valued, "did pangs bring the loved one bliss." A voice then spoke to her at this stage of her yearnings, telling her she was past Rephan and ready for Earth.

If this were all, the expression of the anti-Utopian idea and the valuing of life in all its experiences would make for an interesting variation of the Browning outlook. But it is unfortunate that he also included the speaker's desire to experience death, not because it is an end of things but because it would lead to a "higher sphere" where wrong would test the quality of right and "Who made shall mend." Thus we seem to have come full circle and have the conditions of Rephan all over again. This is a poem that no one quotes and that never gets anthologized.

Browning placed "Reverie" just before the "Epilogue" to *Asolando*, giving it a special prominence, but, alas, it is the least satisfactory poem in the book because it deals in abstractions. Browning's best work presents the voices of men and women speaking of their conflicts of thought, and their actions. When he indulges in philosophical or religious meditations, he seems impelled toward wordiness and his elliptical style becomes more thorny than usual; this not only gets tedious, but it also strays too far away from art. When his men and women are too introspective, we lose sight of them, they become clouded behind their language. This is why his first three long poems, *Pauline*, *Paracelsus*, and *Sordello*, are so seldom read.

In "Reverie" we have the assertion of a characteristic attitude of Browning's about the value of love in life. But instead of appearing in a narrative, a dialogue, or a monologue, it is put in abstract terms in a discussion of the conflict between Power and Love as forces in the world—and by Power, he seems to mean a force that drives the operations of the universe and the workings of history. The speaker looks forward to a time when Power and the mediating force of Love become one. The poem can be interpreted as a religious statement about the power and decrees of God the Father being softened and transformed by the presence of the Son of God, Jesus, but this exalted theme does not make it a successful poem.[9] Indeed, Browning displayed some uncertainties as to just what he did mean in the poem, for the proof-sheets of *Asolando* show that even in the final stage of publication he was making changes in the text—such as putting the capital letters on Power, Love, and Good and substituting "Power" for "Knowledge" in line 173 and "Throe" for "Glory" in line 194. In fact, he made more changes in "Reverie" than in any other poem in the book.[10]

The reverie begins and ends with the same phrasing for the same vision:

> I know there shall dawn a day
> —Is it here on homely earth?
> Is it yonder, world's away,
> Where the strange and the new have birth,
> That Power comes full in play?

Eventually we come to understand that the phrase, "Power comes full in play," means when Power and Love are merged, although the poem describes a long struggle before this takes place. The speaker has faith that this will happen, however, because he feels the development mirrors his own experience in life. He then traces his awakening knowledge in life, from its first perception of the natural world (its recognition of the force he calls Power) on to his discovery that Good is hampered by evil in the world. He wishes that Power would "liberate" and "enlarge Good's strait confine" and put a stop to wrong. To a man's way of thinking, this looks easy if only Love had the kind of limitless sway equal to that of Power.

Yet this is not the way the world runs. The difficulty is that if Good had been able to prevail since the creation of the universe, then perfection would have come too soon. Hence, Power and Love have to be at strife for a developing period while Good struggles to gain strength, as it will in the future.

> Then, life is—to wake not sleep,
>   Rise and not rest, but press
> From earth's level, where blindly creep

Things perfected, more or less,
To the heaven's height, far and steep,

Where, amid what strifes and storms
  May wait the adventurous quest,
Power is Love. . . .

This is the faith that the speaker holds will inevitably take place when "Power comes full in play."

A poem that expresses this kind of blind optimism about the future when the force of Love will reign and takes two hundred twenty lines to do so needs more imagery, analogy, and concrete illustration to hold a reader's interest. One wishes that Browning had avoided indulging his philosophical hopes in meditations like this.

The most successful dramatic monologue in the book, "Imperante Augusto Natus Est—," provides a good literary contrast. This poem in blank verse, that novel form of iambic pentameter that manages still to capture the rhythms of human speech in English, celebrates in a subtle way the triumph of Christianity replacing the reign of Jupiter and his pantheon. "Imperante Augusto Natus Est—" is a companion piece to two dramatic poems in *Men and Women* (1855), "An Epistle Containing the Strange Medical Experience of Karshish" and "Cleon," both of which involve a non-Christian speaker who is not aware of Christian beliefs nor of the developing spread of that religion in the Mediterranean world. Karshish is an Arab. Cleon is a Greek. Now, the speaker in the present poem is a Roman senator. In this work, Browning has drawn on Suetonius's *Lives of the Caesars*

for three important sets of details about Augustus Caesar: he found there the statement that Augustus "could
justly boast" that he had found Rome built of brick but
had left it marble; the description of Augustus's facial
features; and the information that, because of a threaten-
ing dream, Augustus turned beggar once a year and asked
alms of passersby.[11] He also used as a key idea in the poem,
and its title, a prophecy from the *Sibylline Oracles* that a
child would be born in Judea who would become master
of the world, "He was born in the reign of Augustus."[12]

Structurally, the poem is divided into six parts. Part 1
provides an introduction to the scene in the Roman
baths, and the opening question, coming in the middle
of a conversation, sets off the action, "What it was struck
the terror in me?" The answer that the speaker, a Roman
senator, gives develops the entire poem. Line two estab-
lishes the presence of a listener, Publius, to whom the
senator tells what happened yesterday in the baths (part 2)
when the poet Varius read his panegyric on Augustus,
proclaiming that Jupiter would have to vacate his throne
when Augustus died and became a deity. Disgusted with
this exaggerated flattery, the senator goes for a walk in
the streets of Rome, but as he surveys the city, he wonders
how Augustus has managed to avoid the inevitable turn
of the wheel of Fortune. For he sees around him evidences of his power and achievement (part 3), the temples, the Forum, the theater, porticos, the Circus Max-
imus. He remembers the road building, the military
conquests, and the establishment of thirty colonies. He
thinks of the lavish entertainments and the scattering of
donatives to the poor. He acknowledges the extent of the

empire from the Euphrates to the Atlantic and agrees that Varius has his reasons for praise: "No mortal, plainly God!"

Next, Browning includes a hinting reminder (part 4) of the recent birth of Jesus when the senator muses about Augustus who has "this masterdom o'er all the world / Of one who was but born,—like you,—like me, / Like all the world he owns,—of flesh and blood." He wonders how a man with such power looks to the lowest underling, and his eye falls upon a ragged beggar. Godlike indeed must Caesar appear. As he drops a coin into the beggar's palm (part 5), he catches a glimpse of the dark yellowish hair, the hawklike nose, and the eyebrows that meet above it, and he recognizes the face of Augustus himself.

> And terrifyingly into my mind
> Came that quick-hushed report was whispered us,
> "They do say, once a year in sordid garb
> He plays the mendicant, sits all day long,
> Asking and taking alms of who may pass."

This is the way Augustus wards off Fortune's push toward a downfall. The senator now understands the symbolism in the pageantry of a martial triumph when the conqueror has behind him in the chariot an attendant who holds a crown above his head with one hand but points with the other hand down at the conquered leader who crouches in chains at the emperor's feet: "Crown now— Cross when?"—another hint at the ironical means by which Jesus will overcome evil and Christianity will achieve its dominance. "Who stands secure?" the senator asks, "Are even Gods so safe?"

> Jupiter that just now is dominant—
> Are there not ancient dismal tales how once
> A predecessor reigned ere Saturn came,
> And who can say if Jupiter be last?
> Was it for nothing the grey Sibyl wrote
> "Caesar Augustus regnant, shall be born
> In blind Judaea"—one to master him,
> Him and his universe? An old-wife's tale?

The poem has reached its climax and now returns to the scene in the baths (part 6). The senator barks harshly at a slave as he orders the necessary oil, sponge, and strigil. This is the final irony: triumphant Christianity will be the religion of the slaves and of the poor.

In the final poem, the "Epilogue," Browning speaks once more in his own voice, this time addressing his hearers from beyond the grave and offering one more opposition between fancy and fact.[13] Michael Meredith has suggested that the poem is addressed to Katharine Bronson, but since Browning read the poem aloud to Sarianna and Pen's wife, Fannie, shortly before his death, one can justly assume he was speaking to many loved ones whom he would leave behind.[14] He begins,

> At the midnight in the silence of the sleep-time,
>   When you set your fancies free,
> Will they pass to where—by death, fools think, imprisoned—
> Low he lies who once so loved you, whom you loved so,
>   —Pity me?

He rejects such a thought as mistaken, declaring that he never in his life was to be pitied and characterizing himself as the striver and the optimist: "One who never turned his back but marched breast forward, / . . . / Never dreamed, though right were worsted, wrong would triumph."[15] Thus he enjoins his hearers to think of him at noonday, not at midnight and to greet him "with a cheer" and encourage him,

> "Strive and thrive!" cry "Speed,—fight on, fare ever
>   There as here!"

The poem upholds that quality of striving that was an essential in Browning's philosophy of life and was indeed a virtue that the Victorians recognized and responded to in the work of Tennyson and Carlyle and celebrated in their national figures, the captains of industry, the scientific investigators, the leaders of education, and the builders of empire. It was only toward the end of Browning's career that the British public could hear that precept from him as well. Now he would tell them—in addition to his loved ones—that, in his view of the afterlife, which he always regarded as just a spiritual extension of life itself, the striving should continue. In the "Epilogue," he has written his own epitaph.

6

Epilogue to an "Epilogue"

𝒞

What accounts for the creative resurgence of Robert Browning when he was in his mid-seventies? Although there are no exact answers and no accumulation of documentary evidence, one can speculate. It seems most likely to have been his entry once more into the atmosphere of Italy—stimulating in Venice and benign in Asolo—combined with the influence of a new feminine presence that had swung into orbit around his life.

Let us step back and look at the shape of his career to see how true this supposition might be. A view of the whole of Browning's career reveals features that are not common to the careers of other major writers.[1] Most poets have an apprentice period, during which they try to find their voice. Eventually they achieve a style and discover compatible forms, then proceed to develop their mature work. If they live to old age, they decline in creative power, producing either little work or inferior work in their final period. Poets as diverse as Gray, Wordsworth, Tennyson, Arnold, Whitman, and Eliot are examples. It is especially true that very few poets (Hardy, Cummings, and Auden come to mind) retain their creative powers up to the end of a long life.

Both the beginning and the end of Robert Browning's long writing career differed from this pattern. His first three books of poetry, much under the influence of the Romantic movement, were disappointing, being over-wrought in tone and having such stylistic density as to seem obscure to most readers. He then turned to writing verse drama for the stage, and although he mastered his stylistic problems and produced intelligible dialogue, the seven plays he wrote were dramatic failures.

Thus he was thirty years old before he published a short pamphlet entitled "Dramatic Lyrics," which contained, all of a sudden, the two kinds of poems that we think of as characteristic of the Browning mode: short vigorous lyrics or soliloquies and dramatic monologues set in earlier historical periods or in countries outside of England, probing into the psychological recesses of the speakers. A few of the dramatic pieces, "My Last Duchess," "Porphyria's Lover," and "Soliloquy of the Spanish Cloister" had the casualness of language, the irony, the grotesque sensationalism, and the exploration of evil and twisted minds that we now recognize as Browningesque. Other poems, "Count Gismond," "Cristina," and "Incident of the French Camp," had the high-flown romantic idealism of his plays, but it was now controlled and encapsulated in short stanzaic forms.

It had taken him more than a decade to find his true poetic medium. But he seemed to regard these poems as minor poetic flourishes, done with the left hand. He still had hopes of being a Victorian Shakespeare. Unsuccessful on the stage, he published his plays in ill-printed, double-columned pamphlets. At this point of his development, two elements moved into conjunction to change the course of his career—Italy and Elizabeth Barrett.

The great period of Browning's career begins with his second trip to Italy in 1844 and his most fully developed and successful dramatic monologue to date, "The Tomb at St. Praxed's" (later called "The Bishop Orders His Tomb at St. Praxed's Church"), and is followed by his meeting with Miss Barrett, his courtship of her, and their elopement to Italy in 1846. It cannot be mere chance that the love and partnership with Elizabeth, together with the inspiring experience of new surroundings that provided both beauty and haunting historical glories, was coexistent with the period of his mature and enduring literary work written over the next twenty-three years.

Very early in their courtship, Robert submitted his work to Elizabeth for criticism, and he received not only the benefit of her judgment but also, and most important, her encouragement. She was a fellow poet, the first person with whom he felt he could fully communicate, someone who could write to him, "While I live to follow this divine art of poetry . . . in proportion to my love for it and my devotion to it, I must be a devout admirer & student of your works."[2] Moreover, she urged him to aspire to wear the laurels of the great poet of his time: "And I will reverence you both as 'a poet' and '*the* poet'— because it is no false 'ambition' but a right you have—& one which those who live the longest, will see justified to the uttermost."[3]

After Elizabeth's death in 1861, her lingering presence

inspired him long enough to allow him to finish *Dramatis Personae* and to develop and complete *The Ring and the Book*. Even though he had left Italy, the old combination was still potent: *The Ring and the Book* was set in seventeenth-century Italy, and it told, in a series of dramatic monologues, the story of the chivalrous rescue of an entrapped woman and her tragic death; the heroine was clearly modeled on Elizabeth.

After the completion of this masterwork, Robert's creative powers went into decline. The turgid, clouded style of those first three long poems returned, the lack of judgment about plot lines exhibited itself again, and mechanical optimism sometimes intruded into his lyrics. Although Browning published volume after volume of verse, sometimes book-length poems, other times collections of shorter pieces, the new work was inferior to that written during his golden period with Elizabeth under the stimulus of Italy. During the later years he was widely respected, even lionized, yet he seemed to write more from duty and habit than authentic feeling. Years before he had said to Elizabeth, "For every poor speck of a Vesuvius or a Stromboli in my microcosm there are huge layers of ice and pits of black cold water—and I make the most of my two or three fire-eyes, because I know by experience, alas, how these tend to extinction—and the ice grows and grows."[4] The years 1869 to 1886 were Browning's ice age.

He did not return to Italy. He remained working in England, taking any continental holidays with his sister, Sarianna, in France or Switzerland. Then, in 1878, in a sudden nostalgic mood, he decided to show Sarianna the places that had brightened his first youthful visit to Italy in 1838, and they journeyed down from the Alps to the sunny slopes of Asolo and thence to Venice. This psychological Rubicon once crossed, Browning returned to Italy for his autumn holidays almost every year for the remainder of his life—but never to Florence, Lucca, or Rome; all were too intimately hallowed by the spirit of Elizabeth.

It was during this period that the friendship with Katharine Bronson, which began tentatively in 1880, ripened, after repeated visits, into the most important new relationship of his later life. After 1883 Robert and Sarianna were guests either next door to, or in, Ca' Alvisi itself, almost every autumn. It was about this time, Michael Meredith suggests, that Browning began to associate Mrs. Bronson with Elizabeth, wearing the commemorative coin she had given him next to Elizabeth's wedding ring on his watch chain.[5] Also while he was Mrs. Bronson's guest and neighbor at the Palazzo Giustiniani-Recanati, he wrote the "Epilogue" to *Ferishtah's Fancies* (1884), which was addressed to the memory of Elizabeth. Indeed, it is Michael Meredith's publication of Mrs. Bronson's letters, together with his thoughtful "Introduction," that makes clear Browning's unusually warm response to this nurturing new personality. Meredith is certainly right that in these last years Katharine Bronson was filling an emotional void in Browning's life.

Readers of Browning's poetry are the benefactors of this renewal of the happy conjunction of Italy and a woman whose companionship touched him deeply, a situation that, once again, released his creativity. The ice age was over. All but one of the poems in *Asolando* were composed between 1887 and 1889. It is not surprising that Browning would create "Ponte dell' Angelo, Venice" from a story that he read first in Mrs. Bronson's gift volume of Tassini's *Curiositá Venezia* and heard again later during a gondola ride from Luigi, Mrs. Bronson's gondolier. But it is surprising to learn that his sensibilities were so awakened at this time that merely hearing "the birds twittering in the trees" during a carriage ride near Asolo would prompt him to instant composition. Mrs. Bronson tells how he fell silent for a stretch of time and shortly after declared, "I have written a poem since we left Bassano. . . . Oh it is all in my head. I shall write it out presently, as soon as I can find a bit of paper." It was "The Lady and the Painter."[6]

No one will equate all the poems in *Asolando* with those that Browning wrote during his greatest period, but "Development," "Beatrice Signorini," "Imperante Augusto Natus Est—," "Flute-Music with an Accompaniment," "Muckle-Mouth Meg," and the love lyrics could easily take their place in *Men and Women*. Meredith goes so far as to argue that Robert Browning had fallen in love with Katharine Bronson. But if so, Browning was past the point where he could act out his Romantic view of love and seize the moment. More soberly, one must acknowledge the vast body of biographical and literary evidence that he had given his heart away but once and to one woman only. He was speaking of his own permanent bereavement when he gave these lines to the duke in "Parleying with Daniel Bartoli" in 1887.

'T is me his ghost: he died since left and lorn,
As needs must Samson when his hair is shorn.

Some day, and soon, be sure himself will rise,
  Called into life by her who long ago
Left his soul whiling time in flesh-disguise.[7]

APPENDIX

A Selection of Poems from *Asolando*

PROLOGUE

"The Poet's age is sad: for why?
In youth, the natural world could show
No common object but his eye
 At once involved with alien glow—
His own soul's iris-bow.

"And now a flower is just a flower:
 Man, bird, beast are but beast, bird, man—
Simply themselves, uncinct by dower
 Of dyes which, when life's day began,
Round each in glory ran."

Friend, did you need an optic glass,
 Which were your choice? A lens to drape
In ruby, emerald, chrysopras,
 Each object—or reveal its shape
Clear outlined, past escape,

The naked very thing?—so clear
 That, when you had the chance to gaze,
You found its inmost self appear
 Through outer seeming—truth ablaze,
Not falsehood's fancy-haze?

How many a year, my Asolo,
 Since—one step just from sea to land—
I found you, loved yet feared you so—
 For natural objects seemed to stand
Palpably fire clothed! No—

No mastery of mine o'er these!
 Terror with beauty, like the Bush
Burning but unconsumed. Bend knees,
 Drop eyes to earthward! Language? Tush!
Silence 't is awe decrees.

90

And now? The lambent flame is—where?
  Lost from the naked world: earth, sky,
Hill, vale, tree, flower,—Italia's rare
  O'er-running beauty crowds the eye—
But flame? The Bush is bare.

Hill, vale, tree, flower—they stand distinct,
  Nature to know and name. What then?
A voice spoke thence which straight unlinked
  Fancy from fact: see, all 's in ken:
Has once my eyelid winked?

No, for the purged ear apprehends
  Earth's import, not the eye late dazed:
The Voice said "Call my works thy friends!
  At Nature dost thou shrink amazed?
God is it who transcends."

Asolo: Sept. 6, 1889.

DEVELOPMENT

My Father was a scholar and knew Greek.
When I was five years old, I asked him once
"What do you read about?"

                                      "The siege of Troy."
"What is a siege and what is Troy?"

                                          Whereat
He piled up chairs and tables for a town,
Set me a-top for Priam, called our cat
—Helen, enticed away from home (he said)
By wicked Paris, who couched somewhere close
Under the footstool, being cowardly,
But whom—since she was worth the pains, poor puss—
Towzer and Tray,—our dogs, the Atreidai,—sought
By taking Troy to get possession of
—Always when great Achilles ceased to sulk,
(My pony in the stable)—forth would prance
And put to flight Hector—our page-boy's self.
This taught me who was who and what was what:
So far I rightly understood the case
At five years old: a huge delight it proved
And still proves—thanks to that instructor sage
My Father, who knew better than turn straight
Learning's full flare on weak-eyed ignorance,
Or, worse yet, leave weak eyes to grow sand-blind,
Content with darkness and vacuity.

It happened, two or three years afterward,
That—I and playmates playing at Troy's Siege—
My Father came upon our make-believe.
"How would you like to read yourself the tale
Properly told, of which I gave you first
Merely such notion as a boy could bear?

Pope, now, would give you the precise account
Of what, some day, by dint of scholarship,
You'll hear—who knows?—from Homer's very mouth.
Learn Greek by all means, read the Blind Old Man,
Sweetest of singers'—*tuphlos* which means 'blind,'
Hedistos which means 'sweetest.' Time enough!
Try, anyhow, to master him some day;
Until when, take what serves for substitute,
Read Pope, by all means!"

     So I ran through Pope,
Enjoyed the tale—what history so true?
Also attacked my Primer, duly drudged,
Grew fitter thus for what was promised next—
The very thing itself, the actual words,
When I could turn—say, Buttmann to account.

Time passed, I ripened somewhat: one fine day,
"Quite ready for the Iliad, nothing less?
There's Heine, where the big books block the shelf:
Don't skip a word, thumb well the Lexicon!"

I thumbed well and skipped nowise till I learned
Who was who, what was what, from Homer's tongue
And there an end of learning. Had you asked
The all-accomplished scholar, twelve years old,
"Who was it wrote the Iliad?"—what a laugh!
"Why, Homer, all the world knows: of his life
Doubtless some facts exist; it's everywhere:
We have not settled, though, his place of birth:
He begged, for certain, and was blind beside:
Seven cities claimed him—Scio, and best right,
Thinks Byron. What he wrote? Those Hymns we have.
Then there's the 'Battle of the Frogs and Mice,'

That's all—unless they dig 'Margites' up
(I'd like that) nothing more remains to know."

Thus did youth spend a comfortable time;
Until—"What's this the Germans say is fact
That Wolf found out first? It's unpleasant work
Their chop and change, unsettling one's belief:
All the same, while we live, we learn, that's sure."
So, I bent brow o'er *Prolegomena*.

And, after Wolf, a dozen of his like
Proved there was never any Troy at all,
Neither Besiegers nor Besieged,—nay, worse,—
No actual Homer, no authentic text,
No warrant for the fiction I, as fact,
Had treasured in my heart and soul so long—
Ay, mark you! and as fact held still, still hold,
Spite of new knowledge, in my heart of hearts
And soul of souls, fact's essence freed and fixed
From accidental fancy's guardian sheath.
Assuredly thenceforward—thank my stars!—
However it got there, deprive who could—
Wring from the shrine my precious tenantry,
Helen, Ulysses, Hector and his Spouse,
Achilles and his Friend?—though Wolf—ah, Wolf!
Why must he needs come doubting, spoil a dream?

But then "No dream's worth waking"—Browning says:
And here's the reason why I tell thus much.
I, now mature man, you anticipate,
May blame my Father justifiably
For letting me dream out my nonage thus,
And only by such slow and sure degrees
Permitting me to sift the grain from chaff,
Get truth and falsehood known and named as such.

Why did he ever let me dream at all,
Not bid me taste the story in its strength?
Suppose my childhood was scarce qualified
To rightly understand mythology,
Silence at least was in his power to keep:
I might have—somehow—correspondingly—
Well, who knows by what method, gained my gains,
Been taught, by forthrights not meanderings,
My aim should be to loathe, like Peleus' son,
A lie as Hell's Gate, love my wedded wife,
Like Hector, and so on with all the rest.
Could not I have excogitated this
Without believing such men really were?
That is—he might have put into my hand
The "Ethics"? In translation, if you please,
Exact, no pretty lying that improves,
To suit the modern taste: no more, no less—
The "Ethics": 't is a treatise I find hard
To read aright now that my hair is grey,
And I can manage the original.
At five years old—how ill had fared its leaves!
Now, growing double o'er the Stagirite,
At least I soil no page with bread and milk,
Nor crumple, dogsear and deface—boy's way.

SPECULATIVE

Others may need new life in Heaven—
  Man, Nature, Art—made new, assume!
Man with new mind old sense to leaven,
  Nature—new light to clear old gloom,
Art that breaks bounds, gets soaring-room.

I shall pray: "Fugitive as precious—
  Minutes which passed,—return, remain!
Let earth's old life once more enmesh us,
  You with old pleasure, me—old pain,
So we but meet nor part again!"

A PEARL, A GIRL

A simple ring with a single stone
  To the vulgar eye no stone of price:
Whisper the right word, that alone—
  Forth starts a sprite, like fire from ice,
And lo, you are lord (says an Eastern scroll)
Of heaven and earth, lord whole and sole
  Through the power in a pearl.

A woman ('t is I this time that say)
  With little the world counts worthy praise:
Utter the true word—out and away
  Escapes her soul: I am wrapt in blaze,
Creation's lord, of heaven and earth
Lord whole and sole—by a minute's birth—
  Through the love in a girl!

INAPPREHENSIVENESS

We two stood simply friend-like side by side,
Viewing a twilight country far and wide,
Till she at length broke silence. "How it towers
Yonder, the ruin o'er this vale of ours!
The West's faint glare behind it so relieves
Its rugged outline—sight perhaps deceives,
Or I could almost fancy that I see
A branch wave plain—belike some wind-sown tree
Chance-rooted where a missing turret was.
What would I give for the perspective glass
At home, to make out if 't is really so!"
"Has Ruskin noticed here at Asolo
That certain weed-growths on the ravaged wall
Seem" . . . something that I could not say at all,
My thought being rather—as absorbed she sent
Look onward after look from eyes distent
With longing to reach Heaven's gate left ajar—
"Oh, fancies that might be, oh, facts that are!
What of a wilding? By you stands, and may
So stand unnoticed till the Judgment Day,
One who, if once aware that your regard
Claimed what his heart holds,—woke, as from its sward
The flower, the dormant passion, so to speak—
Then what a rush of life would startling wreak

Revenge on your inapprehensive stare
While, from the ruin and the West's faint flare,
You let your eyes meet mine, touch what you term
Quietude—that's an universe in a germ—
The dormant passion needing but a look
To burst into immense life!"
                              "No, the book
Which noticed how the wall-growths wave" said she
"Was not by Ruskin."
                              I said "Vernon Lee?"

NOW

Out of your whole life give but a moment!
All of your life that has gone before,
All to come after it,—so you ignore
So you make perfect the present,—condense,
In a rapture of rage, for perfection's endowment,
Thought and feeling and soul and sense—
Merged in a moment which gives me at last
You around me for once, you beneath me, above me—
Me—sure that despite of time future, time past,—
This tick of our life-time's one moment you love me!
How long such suspension may linger? Ah, Sweet—
The moment eternal—just that and no more—
When ecstasy's utmost we clutch at the core
While cheeks burn, arms open, eyes shut and lips meet!

SUMMUM BONUM

All the breath and the bloom of the year in the bag of
    one bee:
All the wonder and wealth of the mine in the heart of
    one gem:
In the core of one pearl all the shade and the shine of
    the sea:
Breath and bloom, shade and shine,—wonder, wealth,
    and—how far above them—
        Truth, that's brighter than gem,
        Trust, that's purer than pearl,—
Brightest truth, purest truth in the universe—all were
    for me
        In the kiss of one girl.

MUCKLE-MOUTH MEG

Frowned the Laird on the Lord: "So red-handed I catch thee?
  Death-doomed by our Law of the Border!
We've a gallows outside and a chiel to dispatch thee:
  Who trespasses—hangs: all's in order."

He met frown with smile, did the young English gallant:
  Then the Laird's dame: "Nay, Husband, I beg!
He's comely: be merciful! Grace for the callant
  —If he marries our Muckle-mouth Meg!"

"No mile-wide-mouthed monster of yours do I marry:
  Grant rather the gallows!" laughed he.
"Foul fare kith and kin of you—why do you tarry?"
  "To tame your fierce temper!" quoth she.

"Shove him quick in the Hole, shut him fast for a week:
  Cold, darkness and hunger work wonders:
Who lion-like roars now, mouse-fashion will squeak,
  And 'it rains' soon succeed to 'it thunders.'"

A week did he bide in the cold and the dark
  —Not hunger: for duly at morning
In flitted a lass, and a voice like a lark
  Chirped, "Muckle-mouth Meg still ye're scorning?

"Go hang, but here's parritch to hearten ye first!"
"Did Meg's muckle-mouth boast within some
Such music as yours, mine should match it or burst:
  No frog-jaws! So tell folk, my Winsome!"

Soon week came to end, and, from Hole's door set wide,
  Out he marched, and there waited the lassie:
"Yon gallows, or Muckle-mouth Meg for a bride!
  Consider! Sky's blue and turf's grassy:

"Life's sweet: shall I say ye wed Muckle-mouth Meg?"
"Not I," quoth the stout heart: "too eerie
The mouth that can swallow a bubblyjock's egg:
Shall I let it munch mine? Never Dearie!"

"Not Muckle-mouth Meg? Wow, the obstinate man!
Perhaps he would rather wed me!"
"Ay, would he—with just for a dowry your can!"
"I'm Muckle-mouth Meg," chirruped she.

"Then so—so—so—" as he kissed her apace—
"Will I widen thee out till thou turnest
From Margaret Minnikin-mou', by God's grace,
To Muckle-mouth Meg in good earnest!"

BAD DREAMS III

This was my dream: I saw a Forest
  Old as the earth, no track nor trace
Of unmade man. Thou, Soul, explorest—
  Though in a trembling rapture—space
Immeasurable! Shrubs, turned trees,
Trees that touch heaven, support its frieze
Studded with sun and moon and star:
While—oh, the enormous growths that bar
Mine eye from penetrating past
  Their tangled twine where lurks—nay, lives
Royally lone, some brute-type cast
  I' the rough, time cancels, man forgives.

On, Soul! I saw a lucid City
  Of architectural device
Every way perfect. Pause for pity,
  Lightning! nor leave a cicatrice
On those bright marbles, dome and spire,
Structures palatial,—streets which mire
Dares not defile, paved all too fine
For human footstep's smirch, not thine—
Proud solitary traverser,
  My Soul, of silent lengths of way—
With what ecstatic dread, aver,
  Lest life start sanctioned by thy stay!

Ah, but the last sight was the hideous!
  A city, yes,—a Forest, true,—
But each devouring each. Perfidious
Snake-plants had strangled what I knew
Was a pavilion once: each oak
Held on his horns some spoil he broke
By surreptitiously beneath

Upthrusting: pavements, as with teeth,
Griped huge weed widening crack and split
  In squares and circles stone-work erst.
Oh, Nature—good! Oh Art—no whit
  Less worthy! Both in one—accurst!

BEATRICE SIGNORINI

This strange thing happened to a painter once:
Viterbo boasts the man among her sons
Of note, I seem to think: his ready tool
Picked up its precepts in Cortona's school—
That's Pietro Berretini, whom they call
Cortona, these Italians: greatish-small,
Our painter was his pupil, by repute
His match if not his master absolute,
Though whether he spoiled fresco more or less,
And what's its fortune, scarce repays your guess.
Still, for one circumstance, I save his name
—Francesco Romanelli: do the same!
He went to Rome and painted: there he knew
A wonder of a woman painting too—
For she, at least, was no Cortona's drudge:
Witness that ardent fancy-shape—I judge
A semblance of her soul—she called "Desire"
With starry front for guide, where sits the fire
She left to brighten Buonarroti's house.
If you see Florence, pay that piece your vows,
Though blockhead Baldinucci's mind, imbued
With monkish morals, bade folk "Drape the nude
and stop the scandal!" quoth the record prim
I borrow this of: hang his book and him!
At Rome, then, where these fated ones met first,
The blossom of his life had hardly burst
While hers was blooming at full beauty's stand:
No less Francesco—when half-ripe he scanned
Consummate Artemisia—grew one want
To have her his and make her ministrant
With every gift of body and of soul
To him. In vain. Her sphery self was whole—

Might only touch his orb at Art's sole point.
Suppose he could persuade her to enjoint
Her life—past, present, future—all in his
At Art's sole point by some explosive kiss
Of love through lips, would love's success defeat
Artistry's haunting curse—the Incomplete?
Artists no doubt they both were,—what beside
Was she? who, long had felt heart, soul spread wide
Her life out, knowing much and loving well,
On either side Art's narrow space where fell
Reflection from his own speck: but the germ
Of individual genius—what we term
The very self, the God-gift whence had grown
Heart's life and soul's life,—how make that his own?
Vainly his Art, reflected, smiled in small
On Art's one facet of her ampler ball;
The rest, touch-free, took in, gave back heaven, earth,
All where he was not. Hope, well-nigh ere birth
Came to Desire, died of all-unfulfilled.
"What though in Art I stand the abler-skilled,"
(So he conceited: mediocrity
Turns on itself the self-transforming eye)
"If only Art were suing, mine would plead
To purpose: man—by nature I exceed
Woman the bounded: but how much beside
She boasts, would sue in turn and be denied!
Love her? My own wife loves me in a sort
That suits us both: she takes the world's report
Of what my work is worth, and, for the rest,
Concedes that, while his consort keeps her nest,
The eagle soars a licensed vagrant, lives
A wide free life which she at least forgives—
Good Beatricé Signorini! Well

And wisely did I choose her. But the spell
To subjugate this Artemisia—where?
She passionless?—she resolute to care
Nowise beyond the plain sufficiency
Of fact that she is she and I am I
—Acknowledged arbitrator for us both
In her life as in mine which she were loth
Even to learn the laws of? No, and no,
Twenty times over! Ay, it must be so:
I for myself, alas!"

                    Whereon, instead
Of the checked lover's-utterance—why, he said
—Leaning above her easel: "Flesh is red"
(Or some such just remark)—"by no means white
As Guido's practice teaches: you are right."
Then came the better impulse: "What if Pride
Were wisely trampled on, whate'er betide?
If I grow hers, not mine—join lives, confuse
Bodies and spirits, gain not her but lose
Myself to Artemisia? That were love!
Of two souls—one must bend, one rule above:
If I crouch under proudly, lord turned slave,
Were it not worthier both than if she gave
Herself—in treason to herself—to me?"

And, all the while, he felt it could not be.
Such love were true love: love that way who can!
Someone that's born half woman not whole man:
For man, prescribed man better or man worse,
Why, whether microcosm or universe,
What law prevails alike through great and small,
The world and man—world's miniature we call?
Male is the master. "That way"—smiled and sighed

Our true male estimator—"puts her pride
My wife in making me the outlet whence
She learns all Heaven allows: 't is my pretence
To paint: her lord should do what else but paint?
Do I break brushes, cloister me turned saint?
Then, best of all suits sanctity her spouse
Who acts for Heaven, allows and disallows
At pleasure, past appeal, the right, the wrong
In all things. That's my wife's way. But this strong
Confident Artemisia—an adept
In Art does she conceit herself? 'Except
In just this instance,' tell her, 'no one draws
More rigidly observant of the laws
Of right design: yet here,—permit me hint,—
If the acromion had a deeper dint,
That shoulder were perfection.' What surprise
—Nay, scorn, shoots black fire from those startled eyes!
She to be lessoned in design forsooth!
I'm doomed and done for, since I spoke the truth.
Make my own work the subject of dispute—
Fails it of just perfection absolute
Somewhere? Those motors, flexors,—don't I know
Ser Santi, styled 'Tirititototo
The pencil-prig,' might blame them? Yet my wife—
Were he and his nicknamer brought to life,
Tito and Titian, to pronounce again—
Ask her who knows more—I or the great Twain
Our colourist and draughtsman!
                              "I help her,
Not she helps me; and neither shall demure
Because my portion is——" he chose to think—
"Quite other than a woman's: I may drink
At many waters, must repose by none—

Rather arise and fare forth, having done
Duty to one new excellence the more,
Abler thereby, though impotent before
So much was gained of knowledge. Best depart
From this last lady I have learned by heart!"

Thus he concluded of himself—resigned
To play the man and master: "Man boasts mind:
Woman, man's sport calls mistress, to the same
Does body's suit and service. Would she claim
—My placid Beatricé-wife—pretence
Even to blame her lord if, going hence,
He wistfully regards one whom—did fate
Concede—he might accept queen, abdicate
Kingship because of?—one of no meek sort
But masterful as he: man's match in short?
Oh, there's no secret I were best conceal!
Bicé shall know; and should a stray tear steal
From out the blue eye, stain the rose cheek—bah!
A smile, a word 's gay reassurance—ah,
with kissing interspersed,—shall make amends,
Turn pain to pleasure."

                              "What, in truth, so ends
Abruptly, do you say, our intercourse?"
Next day, asked Artemisia: "I'll divorce
Husband and wife no longer. Go your ways
Leave Rome! Viterbo owns no equal, says
The bye-word, for fair women: you, no doubt,
May boast a paragon all specks without,
Using the painter's privilege to choose
Among what's rarest. Will your wife refuse
Acceptance from—no rival—of a gift?
You paint the human figure I make shift

Humbly to reproduce: but, in my hours
Of idlesse, what I fain would paint is—flowers.
Look now!"
                        She twitched aside a veiling cloth
"Here is my keepsake—frame and picture both:
For see, the frame is all of flowers festooned
About and empty space,—left thus, to wound
No natural susceptibility:
How can I guess? 'T is you must fill, not I,
The central space with—her whom you like best!
That is your business, mine has been the rest.
But judge!"
                        How judge them? Each of us, in flowers,
Chooses his love, allies it with past hours,
Old meetings, vanished forms and faces: no—
Here let each favourite unmolested blow
For one heart's homage, no tongue's banal praise,
Whether the rose appealingly bade "Gaze
Your fill on me, sultana who dethrone
The gaudy tulip!" or 't was "Me alone
Rather do homage to, who lily am,
No unabashed rose!" "Do I vainly cram
My cup with sweets, your jonquil?" "Why forget
Vernal endearments with the violet?"
So they contested yet concerted, all
As one, to circle round about, enthral
Yet, self-forgetting, push to prominence
The midmost wonder, gained no matter whence.

There 's a tale extant, in a book I conned
Long years ago, which treats of things beyond
The common, antique times and countries queer
And customs strange to match. "'T is said, last year,"
(Recounts my author,) "that the King had in mind

To view his kingdom—guessed at from behind
A palace-window hitherto. Announced
No sooner was such purpose than 't was pounced
Upon by all the ladies of the land—
Loyal but light of life: they had formed a band
Of loveliest ones but lithest also, since
Proudly they all combined to bear their prince.
Backs joined to breasts,—arms, legs,—nay, ankles, wrists,
Hands, feet, I know not by what turns and twists,
So interwoven lay that you believed
'T was one sole beast of burden which received
The monarch on its back, of breadth not scant
Since with fifty girls made one white elephant."
So with the fifty flowers which shapes and hues
Blent, as I tell, and made one fast yet loose
Mixture of beauties, composite, distinct
No less in each combining flower that linked
With flower to form a fit environment
For—whom might be the painter's heart's intent
Thus, in the midst enhaloed, to enshrine?

"This glory-guarded middle space—is mine?
For me to fill?"
                            "For you, my Friend! We part,
Never perchance to meet again. Your Art—
What if I mean it—so to speak—shall wed
My own, be witness of the life we led
When sometimes it has seemed our souls near found
Each one the other as its mate—unbound
Had your been haply from the better choice
—Beautiful Bicé: 't is the common voice,
The crowning verdict. Make whom you like best
Queen of the central space, and manifest
Your prediliction for what flower beyond

All flowers finds favour with you. I am fond
Of—say—yon rose's rich predominance,
While you—what wonder?—more affect the glance
The gentler violet from its leafy screen
Ventures: so—choose your flower and paint your queen!"

Oh but the man was ready, head as hand,
Instructed and adroit. "Just as you stand,
Stay and be made—would Nature but relent—
By Art immortal!"
     Every implement
In tempting reach—a palette primed, each squeeze
Of oil-paint in its proper patch—with these,
Brushes, a veritable sheaf to grasp!
He worked as he had never dared.
        "Unclasp
My Art from yours who can!"—he cried at length,
As down he threw the pencil—"Grace from Strength
Dissociate, from your flowery fringe detach
My face of whom it frames,—the feat will match
With that of Time should Time from me extract
Your memory, Artemisia!" And in fact,—
What with the pricking impulse, sudden glow
Of soul—head, hand co-operated so
That face was worthy of its frame, 't is said—
Perfect, suppose!
     They parted. Soon instead
Of Rome was home,—of Artemisia—well,
The placid-perfect wife. And it befell
That after the first incontestably
Blessedest of all blisses (—wherefore try
Your patience with embracings and the rest
Due from Calypso's all-unwilling guest

To his Penelope?)—there somehow came
The coolness which as duly follows flame.
So, one day, "What if we inspect the gifts
My Art has gained us?"
                              Now the wife uplifts
A casket-lid, now tries a medal's chain
Round her own lithe neck, fits a ring in vain
—Too loose on the fine finger,—vows and swears
The jewel with two pendant pearls like pears
Betters a lady's bosom—witness else!
And so forth, while Ulysses smiles.
                              "Such spells
Subdue such natures—sex must worship toys
—Trinkets and trash: Yet, ah, quite other joys
Must stir from sleep the passionate abyss
Of—such an one as her I know—not this
My gentle consort with the milk for blood!
Why, did it chance that in a careless mood
(In those days, gone—never to return—
When we talked—she to teach and I to learn)
I dropped a word, a hint which might imply
Consorts exist—how quick flashed fire from eye,
Brow blackened, lip was pinched by furious lip!
I needed no reminder of my slip:
One warning taught me wisdom. Whereas here . . .
Aha, a sportive fancy! Eh, what fear
Of harm to follow? Just a whim indulged!

"My Beatricé, there 's an undivulged
Surprise in store for you: the moment's fit
For letting loose a secret: out with it!
Tributes to worth, you rightly estimate
These gifts of Prince and Bishop, Church and State:
Yet, may I tell you? Tastes so disagree!

There 's one gift, preciousest of all to me,
I doubt if you would value as well worth
The obvious sparkling gauds that men unearth
For toy-cult mainly of you womankind;
Such make you marvel, I concede: while blind
The sex proves to the greater marvel here
I veil to baulk its envy. Be sincere!
Say, should you search creation far and wide,
Was ever face like this?"

              He drew aside
The veil, displayed the flower-framed portrait kept
For private delectation.
              No adept
In florist's lore more accurately named
And praised or, as appropriately, blamed
Specimen after specimen of skill,
Than Bicé. "Rightly placed the daffodil—
Scarcely so right the blue germander. Grey
Good mouse ear! Hardly your auricula
Is powdered white enough. It seems to me
Scarlet not crimson, that anemone:
But there 's amends in the pink saxifrage.
O darling dear ones, let me disengage
You innocents from what your harmlessness
Clasps lovingly! Out thou from their caress,
Serpent!"

         Whereat forth-flashing from her coils
On coils of hair, the *spilla* in its toils
Of yellow wealth, the dagger-plaything kept
To pin its plaits together, life-like leapt
And—woe to all inside the coronal!
Stab followed stab,—cut, slash, she ruined all

The masterpiece. Alack for eyes and mouth
And dimples and endearment—North and South,
East, West, the tatters in a fury flew:
There yawned the circlet. What remained to do?
She flung the weapon, and, with folded arms
And mien defiant of such low alarms
As death and doom beyond death, Bicé stood
Passively statuesque, in quietude
Awaiting judgment.
                                And out judgment burst
With frank unloading of love's laughter, first
Freed from its unsuspected source. Some throe
Must needs unlock love's prison-bars, let flow
The joyance.

                                "Then you ever were, still are,
And henceforth shall be—no occulted star
But my resplendent Bicé, sun-revealed,
Full-rondure! Woman-glory unconcealed,
So front me, find and claim and take your own—
My soul and body yours and yours alone,
As you are mine, mine wholly! Heart's love, take—
Use your possession—stab or stay at will
Here—hating, saving—woman with the skill
To make man beast or god!"

                                And so it proved:
For, as beseemed new godship, thus he loved,
Past power to change, until his dying-day,—
Good fellow! And I fain would hope—some say
Indeed for certain—that our painter's toils
At fresco-spashing, finer stroke in oils,
Were not so mediocre after all;
Perhaps the work appears unduly small

From having loomed too large in old esteem,
Patronized by late Papacy. I seem
Myself to have cast eyes on certain work
In sundry galleries, no judge needs shirk
From moderately praising. He designed
Correctly, nor in colour lagged behind
His age: but both in Florence and in Rome
The elder race so make themselves at home
That scarce we give a glance to ceilingfuls
Of such like as Francesco. Still, one culls
From out the heaped laudations of the time
The pretty incident I put in rhyme.

FLUTE-MUSIC,
WITH AN ACCOMPANIMENT

He. Ah, the bird-like fluting
  Through the ash-tops yonder—
Bullfinch-bubblings, soft sounds suiting
  What sweet thoughts, I wonder?
Fine-pearled notes that surely
  Gather, dewdrop-fashion,
  Deep-down in some heart which purely
  Secretes globuled passion—
Passion insuppressive—
  Such is piped, for certain;
Love, no doubt, nay , love excessive
  'T is, your ash-tops curtain.

Would your ash-tops open
  We might spy the player—
Seek and find some sense which no pen
  Yet from singer, sayer,
Ever has extracted:
  Never, to my knowledge,
Yet has pedantry enacted
  That, in Cupid's College,
Just this variation
  Of the old old yearning
Should by plain speech have salvation,
  Yield new men new learning.

"Love!" but what love, nicely
  New from old disparted,
Would the player teach precisely?
  First of all, he started
In my brain Assurance—
  Trust—entire Contentment—

Passion proved by much endurance;
  Then came—not resentment,
No, but simply Sorrow:
  What was seen had vanished:
Yesterday so blue! To-morrow
  Blank, all sunshine banished.

Hark! 'T is Hope resurges,
  Struggling through obstruction—
Forces a poor smile which verges
  On Joy's introduction.
Now, perhaps, mere Musing:
  "Holds earth such a wonder?
Fairy-mortal, soul-sense-fusing
  Past thought's power to sunder!"
What? calm Acquiescence?
  "Daisied turf gives room to
Trefoil, plucked once in her presence—
  Growing by her tomb, too!"

She. All's your fancy-spinning!
  Here's the fact: a neighbour
Never-ending, still beginning,
  Recreates his labour:
Deep o'er desk he drudges,
  Adds, divides, subtracts and
Multiplies, until he judges
  Noonday-hour's exact sand
Shows the hourglass emptied:
  Then comes lawful leisure,
Minutes rare from toil exempted,
  Fit to spend in pleasure.

Out then with—what treatise?
  Youth's Complete Instructor

How to play the Flute. Quid petis?
  Follow Youth's conductor
On and on, through *Easy*,
  Up to *Harder, Hardest*
Flute-piece, till thou, flautist wheezy,
  Possibly discardest
Tootlings hoarse and husky,
  Mayst expend with courage
Breath—on tunes once bright now dusky—
  Meant to cool thy porridge.

That's an air of Tulou's
  He maltreats persistent,
Till as lief I'd hear some Zulu's
  Bone-piped bag, breath-distent,
Madden native dances.
  I'm the man's familiar:
Unexpectedness enhances
  What your ear's auxiliar
—Fancy—finds suggestive.
  Listen! That's *legato*
Rightly played, his fingers restive
  Touch as if *staccato*.

He. Ah, you trick-betrayer!
  Telling tales, unwise one?
So the secret of the player
  Was—he could surprise one
Well-nigh into trusting
  Here was a musician
Skilled consummately, yet lusting
  Through no vile ambition
After making captive
  all the world,—rewarded

Amply by one stranger's rapture,
  Common praise discarded.

So, without assistance
  Such as music rightly
Needs and claims,—defying distance,
  Overleaping lightly
Obstacles which hinder,—
  He, for my approval,
All the same and all the kinder
  Made mine what might move all
Earth to kneel adoring:
  Took—while he piped Gounod's
Bit of passionate imploring—
  Me for Juliet: who knows?

No! as you explain things,
  All 's mere repetition,
Practice-pother: of all vain things
  Why waste pooh or pish on
Toilsome effort—never
  Ending, still beginning—
After what should pay endeavor
  —Right-performance? winning
Weariness from you who,
  Ready to admire some
Owl's fresh hooting—Tu-whit, tu-who—
  Find stale thrush-songs tiresome.

She. Songs, Spring thought perfection,
  Summer criticizes:
What in May escaped detection,
  August, past surprises,
Notes, and names each blunder.
  You, the just-initiate,

Praise to heart's content (what wonder?)
  Tootings I hear vitiate
Romeo's serenading—
  I who, times full twenty,
Turned to ice—no ash-tops aiding—
  At his *caldamente*.

So, 't was distance altered
  Sharps to flats? The missing
Bar when syncopation faltered
  (You thought—paused for kissing!)
Ash-tops too felonious
  Intercepted? Rather
Say—they well-nigh made euphonious
  Discord, helped to gather
Phrase, by phrase, turn patches
  Into simulated
Unity which botching matches,—
  Scraps redintegrated.

He. Sweet, are you suggestive
  Of an old suspicion
Which has always found me restive
  To its admonition
When it ventured whisper
  "Fool, the strifes and struggles
Of your trembler—blusher—lisper
  Were so many juggles,
Tricks tried—oh, so often!—
  Which once more do duty,
Find again a heart to soften,
  Soul to snare with beauty."

Birth-blush of the briar-rose,
  Mist-bloom of the hedge-sloe,
Someone gains the prize: admire rose

Would he, when noon's wedge—slow—
Sure, has pushed, expanded
　Rathe pink to raw redness?
Would he covet sloe when sanded
　By road-dust to deadness?
So—restore their value!
　Ply a water-sprinkle!
Then guess sloe is fingered, shall you?
　Find in rose a wrinkle?

Here what played Aquarius?
　Distance—ash-tops aiding,
Reconciled scraps else contrarious,
　Brightened stuff fast fading.
Distance—call your shyness:
　Was the fair one peevish?
Coyness softened out of slyness.
　Was she cunning, thievish,
All-but-proved imposter?
　Bear but one day's exile,
Ugly traits were wholly lost or
　Screened by fancies flexile—

Ash-tops these, you take me?
　Fancies' interference
Changed . . .
　　　　　　　　But since I sleep, don't wake me!
What if all 's appearance?
　Is not outside seeming
Real as substance inside?
　Both are facts, so leave me dreaming:
If who loses wins I'd
　Ever lose,—conjecture,
From one phrase trilled deftly,
All the piece. So, end your lecture,
　Let who lied be left lie!

"IMPERANTE AUGUSTO NATUS EST—"

What it was struck the terror in me?
This, Publius: closer! while we wait our turn
I'll tell you. Water's warm (they ring inside)
At the eighth hour, till when no use to bathe.

Here in the vestibule where now we sit,
One scarce stood yesterday, the throng was such
Of loyal gapers, folk all eye and ear
While Lucius Varius Rufus in their midst
Read out that long-planned late-completed piece,
His Panegyric on the Emperor.
"Nobody like him" little Flaccus laughed
"At leading forth an Epos with due pomp!
Only, when godlike Caesar swells the theme,
How should mere mortals hope to praise aright?
Tell me, thou offshoot of Etruscan kings!"
Whereat Maecenas smiling sighed assent.

I paid my quadrans, left the Thermae's roar
Of rapture as the poet asked "What place
Among the godships Jove, for Caesar's sake,
Would bid its actual occupant vacate
In favour of the new divinity?"
And got the expected answer "Yield thine own!"—
Jove thus dethroned, I somehow wanted air,
And found myself a-pacing street and street,
Letting the sunset, rosy over Rome,
Clear my head dizzy with the hubbub—say
As if thought's dance therein had kicked up dust
By trampling on all else: the world lay prone,
As—poet-propped, in brave hexameters—
Their subject triumphed up from man to God.
Caius Octavius Caesar the August—

Where was escape from his prepotency?
I judge I may have passed—how many piles
Of structure dropt like doles from his free hand
To Rome on every side? Why, right and left,
For temples you've the Thundering Jupiter,
Avenging Mars, Apollo Palatine:
How count Piazza, Forum—there 's a third
All but completed. You've the Theatre
Named of Marcellus—all his work, such work!—
One thought still ending, dominating all—
With warrant Varius sang "Be Caesar God!"
By what a hold arrests he Fortune's wheel,
Obtaining and retaining heaven and earth
Through Fortune, if you like, but favour—no!
For the great deeds flashed by me, fast and thick
As stars which storm the sky on autumn nights—
Those conquests! but peace crowned them,—so, of peace!
Count up his titles only—these, in few—
Ten years Triumvir, Consul thirteen times,
Emporer, nay—the glory topping all—
Hailed Father of his Country, last and best
Of titles, by himself accepted so:
And why not? See but feats achieved in Rome—
Not to say, Italy—he planted there
Some thirty colonies—but Rome itself
All new-built, "marble now, brick once," he boasts:
This Portico, that Circus. Would you sail?
He has drained Tiber for you: would you walk?
He straightened out the long Flamimian Way.
Poor? Profit by the score of donatives!
Rich—that is, mirthful? Half-a-hundred games
Challenge your choice! There 's Rome—for you and me
Only? The centre of the world besides!

For, look the wide world over, where ends Rome?
To sunrise? There 's Euphrates—all between!
To sunset? Ocean and immensity:
North,—stare till Danube stops you: South, see Nile,
The Desert and the earth-upholding Mount.
Well may the poet-people each with each
Vie in his praise, our company of swans,
Virgil and Horace, singers—in their way—
Nearly as good as Varius, though less famed;
Well may they cry, "No mortal, plainly God!"

Thus to myself myself said, while I walked:
Or would have said, could thought attain to speech,
Clean baffled by enormity of bliss
The while I strove to scale its heights and sound
Its depths—this masterdom o'er all the world
Of one who was but born,—like you, like me,
Like all the world he owns,—of flesh and blood.
But he—how grasp, how gauge his own conceit
Of bliss to me near inconceivable?
Or—since such flight too much makes reel the brain—
Let's sink—and so take refuge, as it were,
From life's excessive altitude—to life's
Breathable wayside shelter at its base!
If looms thus large this Caesar to myself
—Of senatorial rank and somebody—
How must he strike the vulgar nameless crowd,
Innumerous swarm that 's nobody at all?
Why,—for an instance,—much as yon gold shape
Crowned, sceptred, on the temple opposite—
Fulgurant Jupiter—must daze the sense
Of—say, yon outcast begging from its step!
What, anti-Caesar, monarch in the mud,
As he is pinnacled above thy pate?

Ay, beg away! thy lot contrasts full well
With his whose bounty yields thee this support—
Our Holy and Inviolable One,
Caesar, whose bounty built the fane above!
Dost read my thought? Thy garb, alack, displays
Sore usage truly in each rent and stain—
Faugh! Wash though in Suburra! 'Ware the dogs
Who may not so didsain a meal on thee!
What, stretchest forth a palm to catch my alms?
Aha, why yes: I must appear—who knows?—
I, in my toga, to thy rags and thee—
Quaestor—nay, Ædile, Censor—Pol! perhaps
The very city-Praetor's noble self!
As to me Caesar, so to thee am I?
Good: nor in vain shall prove thy quest, poor rogue!
Hither—hold palm out—take this quarter-as!

And who did take it? as he raised his head,
(My gesture was a trifle—well, abrupt),
Back fell the broad flap of the peasant's-hat,
The homespun cloak that muffled half his cheek
Dropped somewhat, and I had a glimpse—just one!
One was enough. Whose—whose might be the face?
That unkempt careless hair—brown, yellowish—
Those sparkling eyes beneath their eyebrows' ridge
(Each meets each, and the hawk-nose rules between)
—That was enough, no glimpse was needed more!
And terrifyingly into my mind
Came that quick-hushed report was whispered us,
"They do say, once a year in sordid garb
He plays the mendicant, sits all day long,
Asking and taking alms of who may pass,
And so averting, if submission help,
Fate's envy, the dread chance and change of things

When Fortune—for a word, a look, a nought—
Turns spiteful and—the petted lioness—
Strikes with her sudden paw, and prone falls each
Who patted late her neck superiorly,
Or trifled with those claw-tips velvet-sheathed."
"He's God!" shouts Lucius Varius Rufus: "Man
And worms'-meat any moment!" mutters low
Some Power, admonishing the mortal-born.

Ay, do you mind? There's meaning in the fact
That whoso conquers, triumphs, enters Rome,
Climbing the Capitolian, soaring thus
To glory's summit,—Publius, do you mark—
Ever the same attendant who, behind,
Above the Conqueror's head supports the crown
All-too-demonstrative for human wear,
—One hand's employment—all the while reserves
Its fellow, backward flung, to point how, close
Appended from the car, beneath the foot
Of the up-borne exulting Conqueror,
Frown—half-descried—the instruments of shame,
The malefactor's due. Crown, now—Cross, when?

Who stands secure? Are even Gods so safe?
Jupiter that just now is dominant—
Are not there ancient dismal tales how once
A predecessor reigned ere Saturn came,
And who can say if Jupiter be last?
Was it for nothing the grey Sibyl wrote
"Caesar Augustus regnant, shall be born

In blind Judaea"—one to master him,
Him and the universe? An old-wife's tale?

Bath-drudge! Here, slave! No cheating! Our turn next.
No loitering, or be sure you taste the lash!
Two strigils, two oil-drippers, each a sponge!

EPILOGUE

At the midnight in the silence of the sleep-time,
  When you set your fancies free,
Will they pass to where—by death, fools think,
  imprisoned—
Low he lies who once loved you, whom you loved so,
      —Pity me?

Oh to love so, be so loved, yet so mistaken!
  What had I on earth to do
With the slothful, with the mawkish, the unmanly?
like the aimless, helpless, hopeless, did I drivel
      —Being—who?

One who never turned his back but marched breast
      forward,
  Never doubted clouds would break,
Never dreamed, though right were worsted, wrong would
      triumph,
Held we fall to rise, are baffled to fight better,
      Sleep to wake.

No, at noonday in the bustle of man's work-time
  Greet the unseen with a cheer!
Bid him forward, breast and back as either should
      be,
"Strive and thrive!" cry "Speed,—fight on, fare
      ever
      There as here!"

Abbreviations and Cue-Titles

Armstrong • Isobel Armstrong, ed., *Robert Browning*, Writers and Their Background Series (Athens: Ohio University Press, 1974).

Barclay • A. Joseph Armstrong, ed., *Diary of Evelyn Barclay* (Waco, Tex.: Baylor University Browning Interests, Fifth Series, 1937).

Bronson, "Asolo" • Katharine C. de Kay Bronson, "Browning in Asolo," Appendix A, of Michael Meredith, *More Than Friend* (Winfield, Kans.: Wedgestone Press, 1985). Reprinted from *The Century Magazine* 59 (April 1900): 920–31.

Bronson, "Venice" • Katharine C. de Kay Bronson, "Browning in Venice," Appendix B, of Michael Meredith, *More Than Friend* (Winfield, Kans.: Wedgestone Press, 1985). Reprinted from *The Century Magazine* 63 (February 1902), 572–84.

BIS • *Browning Institute Studies* (New York: Browning Institute, 1973–).

BSN • *Browning Society Notes* (London: The Browning Society, 1970–).

De Vane • William Clyde De Vane, *A Browning Handbook*, 2d ed. (New York: Appleton-Century-Crofts, 1955).

Collections • Philip Kelley and Betty Coley, eds., *The Browning Collections, a Reconstruction with Other Memorabilia* (Winfield, Kans.: Wedgestone Press, 1984).

Kintner • *The Letters of Robert Browning and Elizabeth Bar-*

rett Barrett 1845–1846, ed. Evan Kintner (Cambridge: Harvard University Press, 1969).

Korg • Jacob Korg, *Browning in Italy* (Athens: Ohio University Press, 1983).

Miller • Betty Miller, *Robert Browning, A Portrait* (New York: Charles Scribner's Sons, 1953).

MTF • Michael Meredith, *More Than Friend, The Letters of Robert Browning to Katharine de Kay Bronson* (Winfield, Kans.: Wedgestone Press, 1985).

NL • William Clyde De Vane and Kenneth Knickerbocker, eds., *New Letters of Robert Browning* (New Haven: Yale University Press, 1950).

Raymond • William O. Raymond, *The Infinite Moment and Other Essays in Robert Browning* (Toronto: University of Toronto Press, 1950; 2d ed., rev., 1965).

RB • Robert Browning.

Ryals • Clyde de L. Ryals, *Browning's Later Poetry, 1871–1889* (Ithaca: Cornell University Press, 1975).

SBHC • *Studies in Browning and His Circle* (Waco, Tex.: Baylor University, 1973–).

Venezia • Sergio Perosa, ed., *Browning e Venezia* (Firenze: Leo S. Olschki Editore, 1991).

VP • *Victorian Poetry* (Morgantown: University of West Virginia, 1962–).

Williams • Thomas J. Collins, ed., "Letters from Robert Browning to the Reverend J. D. Williams," *BIS* 4 (1976), 1–56.

Notes

1. Westminster Abbey and Asolo

1. Stephen Spender, "Centenary Address, Westminster Abbey, December 12, 1989," *BSN* 20 (Spring 1990): 8.

2. Catalogue: Rosella Mamoli Zorzi, ed., *Robert Browning e Venezia* (Venice: Fondazione Scientifica Quarini Stampalia, 1989).

3. Barclay, 10.

4. Michael Meredith, "Browning and the Prince of Publishers," *BIS* 7 (1979): 1.

5. Details of the memorial funeral service are drawn from "The Burial of Mr. Browning," *Pall Mall Gazette*, December 31, 1889, 4 (rpt. *BIS* 3 [1975]: 119–30), and B. R. Jerman, "The Death of Robert Browning," *University of Toronto Quarterly* 35 (October 1965): 47–74.

6. Among the prominent figures in attendance were literary figures, Henry James, George Meredith, Bret Harte, Rider Haggard, Mrs. Humphry Ward, Mrs. Margaret Oliphant, George Du Maurier, Edmund Gosse, Frank Harris, and Hallam Tennyson (standing in for his father, who was ill); scholars, Benjamin Jowett, David Masson, and Sidney Colvin; historians, James Anthony Froude, William Lecky, Justin McCarthy, and James Bryce; painters, Frederick Leighton, Holman Hunt, and Edward Burne-Jones; editors and publishers, George Smith, William Blackwood, Frederick Macmillan, John Murray, and James Knowles; scientists, Thomas Henry Huxley and Max Müller; the foremost actor of the Victorian stage, Henry Irving; and a large representation of the nobility.

7. Hiram Corson, "A Few Remembrances of Robert Browning," ed. William Peterson, *BIS* 3 (1973): 75. Dr. Corson, a professor at Cornell University, was the founder of the first

Browning Society—in America, four or five years earlier than the London Browning Society was formed in 1881 by Dr. Frederick Furnivall. Dr. Corson was also the author of an early guide to RB's work, *An Introduction to the Study of Robert Browning's Poetry* (Boston: D. C. Heath and Co., 1886).

8. Maisie Ward, *Robert Browning and His World: Two Robert Brownings? (1861–1889)* (New York: Holt, Rinehart and Winston, 1969), 220–26. See also RB's letter to Katharine Bronson, August 8, 1889, *MTF,* 79.

9. For RB's daily routine, see Bronson, "Asolo"; Bronson, "Venice"; Barclay; and Daniel Sargent Curtis, "Robert Browning, 1879 to 1885," Appendix C in *MTF,* 167–79.

10. Williams, 54.

11. Barclay, 5.

12. Lillian Whiting, *The Brownings. Their Life and Art* (Boston: Little, Brown, and Co., 1911), had first given an account of RB's relationship with Katharine Bronson, together with excerpts of many of his letters to her. Now this brief treatment has been completely superseded by *MTF,* which contains a seventy-eight-page "Introduction" describing RB's association with her and a very full annotation of the letters.

13. It is my conjecture that Arthur Bronson left his wife. "Mental breakdown" was a common euphemism at that time to explain a husband's marital infidelity or desertion.

14. Henry James, "Casa Alvisi," *Italian Hours* (New York: Grove Press, 1959), 77.

15. *MTF,* xlvii–xlix.

16. Ibid., 53.

17. Ibid., 97.

18. James, "Italian Hours," 82.

19. Bronson, "Asolo," 132.

20. Ibid., 134. Later Pen Browning bought the property, erected the tower, and called it "Pippa's Tower."

21. Bronson, "Asolo," 140–42. See also RB's singing Russian folksongs with Prince Gagarin, an old Russian expatriate living in Venice. Bronson, "Venice," 156.

22. *MTF,* 102.

23. *NL,* 383.

24. Williams, 56.

25. Henry James, *William Wetmore Story and His Friends* (Boston: Houghton Mifflin Co., 1903), 2:283–84.

26. Barclay, 5.

27. Ibid.

28. Curtis, *MTF*, 173.

29. Barclay, 7.

30. Jerman, "Death," 58.

31. Barclay, 9. She spells the word "syncopy."

32. Ibid.

33. *MTF*, 112.

34. Ibid. This is Pen's report to Katharine Bronson in his exact words. The note card, undated (December 12, 1889), is reproduced photographically. Evelyn Barclay, who was also present, recorded in her diary that the telegram said "that the 1st edition of his book was all sold." She has a somewhat different version, too, of RB's last words. "More than satisfied. I am dying. My dear boy. My dear boy" (9). "Gratifying" and "satisfied" sound very much alike, and "My dear boy" may be easily interpreted from a dying man's murmur. I accept Pen's version of RB's last words. It was he, after all, who was bent over listening to his father's murmur.

2. The Personal Voice

1. In a letter to J. D. Williams, August 28, 1889, RB says, "Asolo is intimately connected with Latinity through Bembo's secretaryship there: his dialogues, *Gli Asolandi*, are in choice Italian, of course: I have them but could never set to work and read them properly" (Williams, 54). *Collections* shows no ownership of this volume, although it records two other books by Bembo, A192 and A193.

2. Thomas Sturge Moore, ed., *Works and Days, From the Journal of Michael Field* (London: John Murray, 1933), 384.

3. Letter, January 9, 1883, Thurman L. Hood, ed., *Letters of Robert Browning Collected by Thomas J. Wise* (New Haven: Yale University Press, 1933), 213.

4. Donald Hair in a very stimulating article "Exploring *Asolando*," *BSN* 8 (April 1978): 3–6, argues that RB actually, and ironically, made no distinction between fact and fancy— that the results of imagination and emotion are also facts. Anthony L. Johnson, however, in some tortured and complex theorizing, "Lyrical Themes and Motifs in *Asolando*," in *Venezia*, 297–323, sees RB as rejecting the Romantic view as illusion and preferring reality, in all the lyric poems in the book, especially as related to what Johnson calls a "four-term" soul and sense relationship between man and woman—with woman as the transformer of man into his best and essential self. Like Johnson, Clyde de L. Ryals, in chapter 12, Ryals, 220–40, feels that in the poems there is "no doubt that the fact is to be preferred to fancy, which includes both dreams and visions," but he later concedes that fact may sometimes need the help of fancy to approach nearer to truth.

5. RB's reference to Wordsworth has been commonly recognized—for example, Hair, Johnson, and Ryals (cited above); Korg, 213; Harold Bloom, "Browning: Good Moments and Ruined Quests," *Poetry and Repression* (New Haven: Yale University Press, 1976), 195; W. David Shaw, "Browning's 'Intimations Ode': The Prologue to *Asolando*," *BSN* 8 (April 1978): 7–8; Lawrence Kramer, "The Intimations Ode and Victorian Romanticism," *VP* 18 (Winter 1980): 315–45; Phillip D. Sharp, "'The Poet's Age is Sad': Browning's Late Reference to Wordsworth," *SBHC* 9 (Fall 1981): 86–91, which also cites "Peter Bell"; and Angelo Righetti, "Releggere *Asolando*," *Venezia*, 273–84.

6. Two especially lucid discussions of nineteenth-century biblical criticism are to be found in Owen Chadwick, "History and the Bible," *The Victorian Church* (New York: Oxford University Press, 1970), 2:40–111; and Basil Willey, "George Eliot: Hennell, Strauss, and Feuerbach" *Nineteenth Century Studies* (London: Chatto and Windus, 1949), 204–36, and "Septum Contra Christum," *More Nineteenth Century Studies* (London: Chatto and Windus, 1956), 137–59.

For RB's response to these ideas in his poetry, see Raymond, 19–51. However, Brahma Chaudhuri maintains in "Browning, Jowett, and English Higher Criticism," *SBHC* 4 (Fall 1976):

119–32, that RB acknowledged the importance of the research of the biblical scholars but still held to the value of Christian principles as the basis for living one's life—a position that was actually similar to that of Professor Benjamin Jowett, one of the contributors to *Essays and Reviews*. RB and Jowett had become close friends after RB was elected an Honorary Fellow of Balliol College, Oxford in 1867.

7. RB's references to Strauss's work, which he probably read in George Eliot's translation, are fairly clear in *Christmas-Eve* (1850). He specifically mentioned *Essays and Reviews* (in "Gold Hair") and Renan (in the "Epilogue") in *Dramatic Personae* (1864). But the only work of biblical criticism in his personal library was John Seeley's *Ecce Homo* (1866), *Collections*, A2064.

8. Philip Drew, "Browning and Philosophy," Armstrong, 104–41, states, "I do not think that *Christmas-Eve and Easter-Day* and 'Development' . . . make much sense unless a reader understands the direction of nineteenth-century criticism of religious evidences. Similarly, 'A Death in the Desert' is in effect a reply to *Wesen des Christentums* of [Ludwig] Feuerbach, which George Eliot translated."

9. "Preface" to *Lyrical Ballads*, 1800.

10. Pierpont Morgan Library, MA1020 V9B.

11. In a recent essay that touches on "Development," Clyde de L. Ryals, "'Development' and the Philosophy of Inadequacy," *BIS* 18 (1990): 23–31, uses the poem as a jumping-off point for a serious discourse on Browning's "philosophy of inadequacy" and, in so doing, attempts to squeeze all of Browning's abundance of idea and attitude into one oversimplified view of life. In his brief discussion of the poem, he puts it under some strain to make it yield this meaning: Browning's "belief that no philosophical point of view, no conceptual framework, no demonstrative proof—however persuasive it might be—can ever be adequate by itself."

12. Edward C. McAleer, ed., *Dearest Isa: Robert Browning's Letters to Isabella Blagden* (Austin: University of Texas Press, 1951), 267.

13. Miller, 298, connects this poem, however, with Katharine Bronson.

3. Aspects of Love

1. Most of the critical commentary on RB's love poetry focuses on individual poems. Older discussions that do range widely over the love poetry, such as Edward Dowden's *Robert Browning* (London: J. M. Dent, 1904) do no more than lump the poems into thematic categories—say, poems of attainment in love, poems of failure in love. A few discussions, however, stand out, for example, George Santayana's famous attack "The Poetry of Barbarism," *Interpretations of Poetry and Religion* (New York: Scribner, 1900), 188–216, in which he objects to RB's glorification of "the irrationality of the passions." The only important recent study is Isobel Armstrong's brilliant analysis in "Browning and the Victorian Poetry of Sexual Love," Armstrong, 267–98, in which she declares, "Browning's love lyrics turn out to be passionately about intertwined emotional-psychological problems, and this puts him directly inside the Romantic tradition. His concerns are the concerns, transmuted by his dazzling, sensory intelligence, of his great Romantic precursors—solipsism, fantasy, identity, the action and reaction of past with present. He is the most directly Romantic of all the Victorian poets, and so his response to sexual love is coloured by Romantic ideas, rather than the problems with which his contemporaries are concerned." She feels, however, and this is curious in such a perceptive critical study, that the important love poems do not continue after *Men and Women* (1855).

2. Daniel Karlin, "*Asolando* and the Browning Love Letters," *BSN* 8 (April 1978): 7–8, has found a source for "Which?" in a letter in which Elizabeth describes an occasion at which three women talked together about love and how best to achieve it.

3. Horatius Flaccus, Epodes 5 and 17. In a letter to Felix Moscheles, May 9, 1889, *NL*, 375, RB makes reference to "the old Canidia-type of witch-hood," not the good or "white" witchcraft.

4. In "Portrait of a Dream: A Brief Study of Browning's *Rosny*," *BSN* 9 (April 1979): 3–4, Stephen Garrison states,

"The poem owes its obscurity to the extreme compactness of the lines and the eccentric punctuation, especially around the refrain that comprises the second line of each stanza." Garrison's interpretation, however, that the poem is a dream does not clear up any of its difficulties.

5. The only study of this concept, "The Infinite Moment," in Raymond, 3–18, fails to deal with the complexity of Browning's philosophy of love.

6. RB's position that it is right to take action in matters of love even though it may lead to an adulterous union was one of Santayana's points in accusing him of Romantic barbarism. In a defense and explanation of RB's views, W. O. Raymond, "Browning's 'The Statue of the Bust,'" in the second edition of Raymond, 214–23, rectified some of the shortcomings of his earlier essay (see footnote 5 of this chapter).

7. Evelyn Barclay records that RB pronounced the title "Muckle Moo'ed Meg" in his public reading, Barclay, 6.

8. *MTF,* lviii, and Miller, 297. Malcolm Hicks, "Communication Problems in 'Inapprehensiveness,'" *BSN* 7 (July 1977): 59–62, rejects Miller's implied criticism of RB for failing to respond to Mrs. Bronson's readiness to love him. He sensibly regards the poem as an artistic work in which RB's idea reflects on both the speaker and the woman for their inapprehensiveness.

I should point out that Browning has failed to supply quotation marks at the end of line 11 and the beginning of line 12, but I have added them. Although he made many changes in punctuation in the page proofs of *Asolando,* he did not correct the missing quotation marks in this poem. He overlooked their absence, I believe, because in the page proofs, the woman's speech reaches the bottom of the page at line 11, and the man's reply begins at the top of the facing page. See my forthcoming article, "A Necessary Emendation in Browning's 'Inapprehensiveness.'"

9. The authoritative study of religious mysticism is Evelyn Underhill, *Mysticism, A Study in the Nature and Development of Man's Spiritual Consciousness* (London: Methuen, 1911, and later editions). Aldous Huxley, *The Perennial Philosophy* (New York:

Harper and Brothers, 1945) goes beyond this to make clear the common ground in religion, philosophy, and literature of the psychological experience described in such diverse movements as Hinduism, Taoism, Buddhism, Platonism, Islamic Sufism, Medieval Christianity, Quakerism, New England Transcendentalism, and Wordsworthian Pantheism.

The one study of mysticism in RB's work, F. R. G. Duckworth, *Browning, Background and Conflict* (New York: E. P. Dutton, 1932), chapter 8, 162–82, fails to come to grips with this phenomenon in RB's poems, although Duckworth does recognize the tendency in several works and the specific experience handled in both "Saul" and "By the Fireside." Duckworth, who focuses almost entirely on religious mysticism, feels that RB does not show sufficiently the interpenetration of the two realms, "the eternal and the infinite with the temporal and the finite" necessary to be called a genuine mystic.

10. Pietro De Logu, "Il tema della morte in *Asolando*," *Venezia*, 287, who interprets all of the poems in *Asolando* as reflecting aspects of death, reads "Now" as a desire to suspend time because of the approach of death. Anthony L. Johnson, "Lyrical Themes and Motifs in *Asolando*," *Venezia*, 317–19, sees "Now" as addressed to Katharine Bronson and even finds an anagram of repeated letters (N, O, S, R) in the poem, which he suggests spells out her name, especially in the last line.

11. I find it very strange that Ryals, 239, and Roma King, *The Focusing Artifice, The Poetry of Robert Browning* (Athens: Ohio University Press, 1968), 234, think the "Bad Dreams" group to be the best poems in *Asolando*.

12. Donald Thomas, *Robert Browning, A Life Within a Life* (New York: Viking Press, 1982) pays attention only to "Bad Dreams" in *Asolando*, for he thinks that the other poems merely reflect RB's optimism. He sees the sequence as representative of RB's interest in human psychology. On "Bad Dreams II" he observes, "On the whole, the poem offers an astute insight into the way in which a dream may reveal to a man his subconscious feelings about the woman whom he loves" (283). His critical view of the poems is about on this level.

13. De Vane, 532.

14. Ryals, 239, interprets this poem biographically: RB, seen as shedding tears over his wife's grave, is feeling guilt about his proposal of marriage to Lady Ashburton. On the contrary, if we were to venture any biographical suggestion at all, the text would invite us to think of RB's possible regret over criticizing Elizabeth for her belief in spiritualism and her confidence in seances and spiritualist mediums.

4. Art as Perspective

1. De Vane, 512–13.

2. RB's defense of painting the nude was partly a standing up for the work of his son, Pen. Recently, a sculpted nude by Pen had not been accepted for an exhibition in Burlington House because of the objections of the treasurer of the Royal Academy, John Callot Horsley, an opponent of the nude in art. Barbara Arnett Melchiori, "Beatrice Signorini," *BSN* 7 (December 1977): 81.

3. RB was intrigued by a rhyming closure in a poem by Francis Quarles. In a letter to Mrs. Bronson, September 6, 1884, he wrote, "By the way, what is the most emphatic close of any verse I ever read, if not this which *you* shall read. It occurs at the end of the first of Quarles' Emblems—a beloved book of my boyhood. There is a dialogue between the Serpent and Eve: arguments for plucking the apple and letting it alone: at last Eve decides—

Eve: 'I'll pluck, and taste, and tempt my Adam too
                To try the virtues of this apple.'
Serpent: 'Do!'" (*MTF*, 52–53).

4. RB was very active in the antivivisection movement. He was the vice-president of the Victoria Street Society for the Protection of Animals.

A very brief poem in *Asolando*, "Arcades Ambo," promotes an antivivisection theme. The title, meaning "Arcadians Both," is ironical, since the two stanzas present the statements of two cowards: the first, a speaker who had run away from a battle; the second, a speaker who suffers from gout but who also admits that he is a person "who would have no end of brutes / Cut up alive to guess what suits / My case and saves my toe from shoots."

5. The best-known prose statement of this idea is found in John Ruskin, "The Nature of Gothic," chapter 6 in *The Stones of Venice*, 1851.

6. De Vane, 542–43, outlines RB's source for the story as Baldinucci's *Notizie* once more. But additional specific detail is supplied by Melchiori, "Beatrice Signorini," 87, n. 2.

7. Ibid., 83. Melchiori reads the relationship between Romanelli and Artemesia as reflecting a male-female bristling that she conjectures took place when Robert and Elizabeth criticized each other's work.

8. Ibid., 86. Two recent discussions of "Beatrice Signorini" focus on thematic significance. In spite of all her sound research into the background of the poem, Melchiori's feminist reading of the poem is disappointingly topsy-turvy. She sees the work as an expression of RB's resentful male assertiveness in reply to the Victorian feminist movement. On the other hand, John G. Rudy, "Browning's 'Beatrice Signorini' and the Problems of Aesthetic Aspiration," *BSN* 7 (December 1977): 87–93, offers a valuable reading tied to the ideas about art that the poem suggests. He sees a central theme: "the need to reconcile the ideals of aesthetic aspiration to the conditions of the ordinary world." Romanelli had been inspired by Artemesia to paint the only masterpiece of his whole career, but Beatricé's destruction of it brings him back to the valuing of life over art.

9. Katharine Bronson describes the origin of RB's poem as follows (Bronson, "Venice," 157). He first found the legend in Giuseppi Tassini's *Curiositá Venezia ovvero Origini delle denominazioni stradali di Venezia, 1887*, a book that she had given him as a gift, December 10, 1888 (*Collections*, A2248). He checked the story further in Boviero's *Annals of the Cappucini*. Finally, and this accounts for the liveliness of tone that RB adopted for the poem, he heard from Mrs. Bronson's gondolier, Luigi, the version that Venice preserved in oral tradition. In the manuscript the poem is dated January 9, 1889.

De Vane, 541, gives a translation of Tassini's entry in *Curi-osità Venezia*.

10. C. Castan, "Browning's 'Flute-Music, with an Accompaniment' as a Love Drama," *BSN* 7 (March 1977): 4–11. She also identifies the author of the exercise book that RB mentions in the poem, *Youth's Complete Instructor/How to Play the Flute*, as Jean Louis Tulou.

11. Castan makes a valuable observation that the form of the poem is "a cross between a dialogue and a dramatic monologue," which she labels a "dramatic duologue." She points out that it differs from a dramatic monologue in that the listener does not remain silent.

12. George Ridenour, "Browning's Music Poems," *PMLA* 78 (1963): 369–77 (Rpt. in Clarence Tracy, ed., *Browning's Mind and Art* [Edinburgh: Oliver and Boyd, 1968], 163–83) discusses a series of RB's poems in order to set forth his ideas on music, but in commenting on this poem, he does not perceive the revelation, gradually developed, between the man and the woman.

5. Religion and Power

1. RB's parents attended the York Street Chapel in Walworth, where RB was baptized on June 14, 1812. A plaque in the building identified the spot at which he "worshipped in his boyhood and youth." I am informed that the building, a theatrical warehouse when I visited it in 1970, has since been pulled down. One may become familiar with the liberal Calvinism preached by the minister of the chapel in the book *A Course of Sermons on Faith and Practice delivered by the Rev. George Clayton at York Street Chapel, Walworth 1838–39* (London, 1839). For an account of Clayton, see Thomas W. Aveling, *Memorials of the Clayton Family* (London: Jackson, Walford, and Hodder, 1867).

2. For an excellent treatment of RB's religious upbringing, see John Maynard, "Robert Browning's Evangelical Background," *BIS* 3 (1975): 1–16, which is reprinted in his book, *Browning's Youth* (Cambridge: Harvard University Press, 1977),

51–61. Shorter accounts may be found in the principal biographies, Maisie Ward, *Robert Browning and His World: The Private Face* (New York: Holt, Rinehart and Winston, 1967) and William Irvine and Park Honan, *The Book, The Ring, and the Poet* (New York: McGraw-Hill, 1974). My own research in this area is not yet published.

3. Before RB's settlement in Italy, there was a distinct anti-Catholic coloration in several of his early poems. For a frank discussion of this, see Barbara Melchiori, "Browning in Italy," Armstrong, 168–83, but her pronouncement is "Browning's attitude to Catholicism, as to most things, was contradictory."

4. There is considerable controversy on this point. I tend to agree with Robert Langbaum, "Is Guido Saved?" *VP* 10 (1972): 289–305, rather than with his opponents, Dalton H. Gross, "Browning's Positivist Count in Search of a Miracle: A Grim Parody in *The Ring and the Book*," *VP* 12 (1974): 178–80; James F. Loucks, "'Guido Hope?': A Response to 'Is Guido Saved?'" *SBHC* 2 (Fall 1974): 37–48; and Boyd Litzinger, "The New Vision of Judgment: The Case of St. Guido," *Tennessee Studies in Literature* 20 (1975): 69–75.

5. De Vane, 535–36.

6. Korg, 213, states, however, that the poem is based on an anecdote about Sixtus V "which Browning may have read in a biography by Gregorio Leti"—but, he adds, "is primarily Browning's invention."

7. RB explains in a note that the idea came from a prose story by Jane Taylor. De Vane, 549–51, describes her children's story, "How It Strikes a Stranger," and he also notes that RB took the name "Rephan" from *Acts* 7:43.

8. "Give me your tired, your poor, / Your huddled masses yearning to breathe free, / The wretched refuse of your teeming shore, / Send these, the homeless, tempest-tossed to me: /

I lift my lamp beside the golden door," Emma Lazarus, "The New Colossus": inscription for the Statue of Liberty, New York Harbor.

9. For summary and discussion of RB's elusive religious views in his later years, Henry Jones, *Browning as a Philosophical and Religious Teacher* (New York: Macmillan, 1891) is still valu-

able. Among recent studies, two may be recommended: Kingsbury Badger, "'See the Christ Stand!' Browning's Religion," *Boston University Studies in English* 1 (1955–1956): 53–73, and William Whitla, *The Central Truth: The Incarnation in Browning's Poetry* (Toronto: University of Toronto Press, 1963).

10. Pierpont Morgan Library, bound proof-copy of *Asolando*, 24061 W17D.

11. Tranquillus Suetonius, "Augustus." Sections 28, 29, 30, 40, 43, 46, 79, 91, and 94, *Lives of the Caesars*. RB had an English translation by A. Thomson (London, 1796) in his library. *Collections*, A2229.

12. De Vane, 345–46.

13. One of the best known of RB's poems, the "Epilogue" is often seen as a valedictory companion piece with Tennyson's "Crossing the Bar," which was published the same year. Although it has been widely loved and admired, some critics reacting against its popularity have dismissed it as "mere rhetoric" or "typical Browning optimism." Many early commentators, not reading the text carefully, assumed it was addressed to Elizabeth, but a close scrutiny makes evident that it is addressed to a living person or persons.

14. *MTF*, lxiii and lxvi. The reading aloud was reported in the *Pall Mall Gazette*, February 1, 1890.

15. The quality of inspiration that the poem holds, together with the eeriness of its being spoken from the other side of death has appealed especially to soldiers. During the Boer War, Violet Hunt quoted this stanza while giving a talk at a military camp and reported a surprising response: "I was promptly asked to say it over again slowly; pencils and odd scraps of paper were produced, and all over the tent I saw laborious efforts being made to scribble down the verse. The audience included yeomanry, C.I.V.'s, gunners, sappers, and men from three or four line battalions. I suggested it would be better to wait until the close of the evening, when those who wished for the verse could stay behind, and I would dictate it as slowly as they wished. When the time came, more than three hundred men left their places, and carried away the words pencilled inside pocket Testaments, note-books, on the backs of envelopes, or on any piece

of paper that could be raised." Letter to the *Spectator*, October 25, 1902 (quoted in *The Browning Collections*, 1913, the catalogue of Sotheby, Wilkinson, and Hodge, issued for the auction of the Estate of Robert Barrett Browning, 44–45). It probably evoked the same response in World War I: Paul Fussell, *The Great War and Modern Memory* (London: Oxford University Press, 1975), 159, states that "the *Oxford Book of English Verse* [which contained the "Epilogue"] presides over the Great War in a way that has never been sufficiently appreciated."

6. EPILOGUE TO AN "EPILOGUE"

1. I wish to acknowledge the stimulus to my thinking about Browning's career that resulted from my reading Lawrence Lipking's *The Life of the Poet: Beginning and Ending Poetic Careers* (Chicago: University of Chicago Press, 1981), even though he does not discuss Browning.

2. Kintner, 1:5.

3. Ibid., 1:79.

4. Ibid., 1:75.

5. *MTF*, xlv.

6. Bronson, "Asolo," 132.

7. Lines 334–38.

Index